TEACHER'S PET PUBLICATIONS

## LITPLAN TEACHER PACK
for
### Flowers for Algernon
based on the book by
Daniel Keyes

Written by
Barbara M. Linde, MA Ed.

© 1996 Teacher's Pet Publications
All Rights Reserved

This **LitPlan** for Daniel Keys'
*Flowers For Algernon*
has been brought to you by Teacher's Pet Publications, Inc.

Copyright Teacher's Pet Publications 1996

Only the student materials in this unit plan (such as worksheets,
study questions, and tests) may be reproduced multiple times
for use in the purchaser's classroom.

For any additional copyright questions,
contact Teacher's Pet Publications.

www.tpet.com

# TABLE OF CONTENTS - *Flowers for Algernon*

| | |
|---|---|
| Introduction | 5 |
| Unit Objectives | 7 |
| Unit Outline | 8 |
| Reading Assignment Sheet | 9 |
| Study Questions | 13 |
| Quiz/Study Questions (Multiple Choice) | 26 |
| Pre-Reading Vocabulary Worksheets | 43 |
| Lesson One (Introductory Lesson) | 59 |
| Nonfiction Assignment Sheet | 63 |
| Oral Reading Evaluation Form | 65 |
| Writing Assignment 1 | 67 |
| Writing Evaluation Form | 68 |
| Writing Assignment 2 | 71 |
| Extra Writing Assignments/Discussion ?s | 74 |
| Writing Assignment 3 | 79 |
| Vocabulary Review Activities | 80 |
| Unit Review Activities | 82 |
| Unit Tests | 89 |
| Unit Resource Materials | 121 |
| Vocabulary Resource Materials | 135 |

# A FEW NOTES ABOUT THE AUTHOR
## DANIEL KEYES

KEYES, Daniel 1927- Award winning author Daniel Keyes was born on August 9, 1927, in Brooklyn, New York. He grew up in New York City and attended the public schools there. Keyes attended college for one year, then joined the Marines.

When his tour of duty with the Marines was completed, Daniel Keyes attended Brooklyn College and earned a B. A. in psychology. In 1950 he went to work for a magazine firm in New York as an associate fiction editor. He stayed there for one year, then went into the photography business. This career lasted only a short time, and in 1954 Keyes began teaching English at the high school which he had attended.

During the next several years, Keyes taught during the day, went to Brooklyn College at night to pursue a Master's degree in English and American Literature, and wrote on the weekends. In 1962 he joined the faculty at Wayne State University in Detroit, Michigan, as an instructor in English. He taught there until 1966. From 1966-1972, he was a lecturer at Ohio University in Athens, Ohio. In 1972 Keyes became a professor of English at Ohio University.

*Flowers for Algernon* is Keyes most well-known work. It was originally written as a short story. In 1959, the short story version was awarded the Hugo Award at the World Science Fiction Convention. Keyes was encouraged to develop the short story into a novel. This novel version of *Flowers for Algernon* received the Nebula Award from the Science Fiction Writers of America in 1966. Keyes also received the Mystery Writers of America special award for *The Minds of Billy Milligan*.

In 1961, the CBS Playhouse aired "The Two Worlds of Charlie Gordon," a television play based on the short story "Flowers for Algernon." "Charly," the film version of the novel *Flowers for Algernon,* was released in 1968. Actor Cliff Robertson starred as Charlie Gordon. *Flowers for Algernon* has also been adapted for the live stage, and has been produced in Canada, England, and the United States.

Keyes's other writings include *The Touch,* 1968; *The Fifth Sally*, 1980; and *The Minds of Billy Milligan* (nonfiction), 1981.

Daniel Keyes lives in Athens, Ohio.

# INTRODUCTION

This unit has been designed to develop students' reading, writing, thinking, listening and speaking skills through exercises and activities related to *Flowers for Algernon* by Daniel Keyes. It includes nineteen lessons, supported by extra resource materials.

The **introductory lesson** introduces students to the plight of the main character in the novel through a hands-on activity. Following the introductory activity, students are given an explanation of how the activity relates to the book they are about to read.

The **reading assignments** are approximately thirty pages each; some are a little shorter while others are a little longer. Students have approximately 15 minutes of pre-reading work to do prior to each reading assignment. This pre-reading work involves reviewing the study questions for the assignment and doing some vocabulary work for 8 to 12 vocabulary words they will encounter in their reading.

The **study guide questions** are fact-based questions; students can find the answers to these questions right in the text. These questions come in two formats: short answer or multiple choice. The best use of these materials is probably to use the short answer version of the questions as study guides for students (since answers will be more complete), and to use the multiple choice version for occasional quizzes. It might be a good idea to make transparencies of your answer keys for the overhead projector.

The **vocabulary work** is intended to enrich students' vocabularies as well as to aid in the students' understanding of the book. Prior to each reading assignment, students will complete a two-part worksheet for approximately 8 to 12 vocabulary words in the upcoming reading assignment. Part I focuses on students' use of general knowledge and contextual clues by giving the sentence in which the word appears in the text. Students are then to write down what they think the words mean based on the words' usage. Part II gives students dictionary definitions of the words and has them match the words to the correct definitions based on the words' contextual usage. Students should then have an understanding of the words when they meet them in the text.

After each reading assignment, students will go back and formulate answers for the study guide questions. Discussion of these questions serves as a **review** of the most important events and ideas presented in the reading assignments.

After students complete extra discussion questions, there is a **vocabulary review** lesson which pulls together all of the separate vocabulary lists for the reading assignments and gives students a review of all of the words they have studied.

Following the reading of the book, two lessons are devoted to the **extra discussion questions/writing assignments**. These questions focus on interpretation, critical analysis and personal response, employing a variety of thinking skills and adding to the students' understanding of the novel. These questions are done as a **group activity**. Using the information they have acquired so far through individual work and class discussions, students get together to further examine the text and to brainstorm ideas relating to the themes of the novel.

The group activity is followed by a **reports and discussion** session in which the groups share their ideas about the book with the entire class; thus, the entire class gets exposed to many different ideas regarding the themes and events of the book.

There are three **writing assignments** in this unit, each with the purpose of informing, persuading, or having students express personal opinions. The first assignment is to **persuade.** Students will persuade a doctor that they should be chosen to receive an experimental procedure designed to make them smarter. The second assignment is to **inform**. Students will write a news story based on Charlie's operation. The third assignment is to give a **personal opinion**. Students will give their opinion on using science and technology to alter the human condition.

In addition, there is a **nonfiction reading assignment**. Students are required to read a piece of nonfiction related in some way to *Flowers for Algernon*. After reading their nonfiction pieces, students will fill out a worksheet on which they answer questions regarding facts, interpretation, criticism, and personal opinions. During one class period, students make **oral presentations** about the nonfiction pieces they have read. This not only exposes all students to a wealth of information, it also gives students the opportunity to practice **public speaking**.

The **review lesson** pulls together all of the aspects of the unit. The teacher is given four or five choices of activities or games to use which all serve the same basic function of reviewing all of the information presented in the unit.

The **unit test** comes in two formats: all multiple choice-matching-true/false or with a mixture of matching, short answer, and composition. As a convenience, two different tests for each format have been included.

There are additional **support materials** included with this unit. The **extra activities packet** includes suggestions for an in-class library, crossword and word search puzzles related to the novel, and extra vocabulary worksheets. There is a list of **bulletin board ideas** which gives the teacher suggestions for bulletin boards to go along with this unit. In addition, there is a list of **extra class activities** the teacher could choose from to enhance the unit or as a substitution for an exercise the teacher might feel is inappropriate for his/her class. **Answer keys** are located directly after the **reproducible student materials** throughout the unit. The student materials may be reproduced for use in the teacher's classroom without infringement of copyrights. No other portion of this unit may be reproduced without the written consent of Teacher's Pet Publications, Inc.

## UNIT OBJECTIVES  *Flowers for Algernon*

1. Through reading *Flowers for Algernon,* students will analyze characters and their situations to better understand the themes of the novel.

2. Students will demonstrate their understanding of the text on four levels: factual, interpretive, critical, and personal.

3. Students will practice reading aloud and silently to improve their skills in each area.

4. Students will enrich their vocabularies and improve their understanding of the novel through the vocabulary lessons prepared for use in conjunction with it.

5. Students will answer questions to demonstrate their knowledge and understanding of the main events and characters in *Flowers for Algernon.*

6. Students will practice writing through a variety of writing assignments.

7. The writing assignments in this are geared to several purposes:
    a. To check the students' reading comprehension
    b. To make students think about the ideas presented by the novel
    c. To make students put those ideas into perspective
    d. To encourage critical and logical thinking
    e. To provide the opportunity to practice good grammar and improve students' use of the English language.

8. Students will read aloud, report, and participate in large and small group discussions to improve their public speaking and personal interaction skills.

## UNIT OUTLINE *Flowers for Algernon*

| 1<br><br>Unit Intro<br>Distribute Unit Materials<br>PV 1-8 | 2<br><br>Read 1-8<br>Study?s 1-8<br>Nonfiction Ass't. | 3<br><br>PVR 9-10<br>Oral Reading Eval. | 4<br><br>Quiz 1-10<br>PVR 11 | 5<br><br>Writing Assignment 1 |
|---|---|---|---|---|
| 6<br><br>Study ?s 11<br>PVR 12-13 | 7<br><br>Study ?s 12-13<br>PVR 14 | 8<br><br>Study?s 14<br>Writing Assignment 2 | 9<br><br>Writing Conference | 10<br><br>PVR 15-16<br>Study ?s 15-16 |
| 11<br><br>PVR 17<br>Study ?s 17 | 12<br><br>Extra Discussion ?s | 13<br><br>Writing Assignment 3 | 14<br><br>Library Work | 15<br><br>Vocab Review |
| 16<br><br>Movie & Discuss | 17<br><br>Non-Fiction Ass't. | 18<br><br>Unit Review | 19<br><br>Unit Test | |

Key: P=Preview Study Questions   V=Vocabulary Worksheet   R=Read

# READING ASSIGNMENT SHEET
*Flowers for Algernon*

| Date Assigned | Chapters (Progress Reports) | Complete By Date |
|---|---|---|
|  | 1-8 |  |
|  | 9-10 |  |
|  | 11 |  |
|  | 12-13 |  |
|  | 14 |  |
|  | 15-16 |  |
|  | 17 |  |

# STUDY QUESTIONS

## SHORT ANSWER STUDY QUESTIONS  *Flowers For Algernon*

Progress Reports 1-8
1. How is the novel written?
2. Describe the main character.
3. What kind of test did Burt give Charlie? What was the result?
4. Why was Charlie taking the tests?
5. What did Miss Kinnian, Charlie's teacher, tell the doctors about him?
6. What happened when Charlie was given the Thematic Apperception Test?
7. Who was Algernon? Describe Charlie's first meeting with him.
8. What was Professor Nemur worried about with regard to the operation?
9. Why did Charlie want to be smart?
10. What was Mr. Donner's relationship with Charlie?
11. How did Charlie feel after the operation, and how did the doctors help him?
12. How long after the surgery was it when Charlie began to see results, and what were they?

Progress Reports 9-10
1. Describe what happened at the bakery on April Fool's Day.
2. What did Charlie discover at the party he went to with Joe and Frank?
3. How did Charlie know he was getting smarter?
4. To whom did Charlie talk about his memories and dreams, and why?
5. Describe what happened when Burt administered the Rorschach test to Charlie.
6. How were Mr. Donner and the other employees at the bakery reacting to Charlie?
7. What was Charlie's IQ at this point in the story?
8. What happened when Charlie overheard Nemur and Strauss discussing the presentation of their findings?
9. What concerned Charlie about making friends with some of the boys at the Campus Bowl?
10. Describe Charlie's dream about P.S. 13. Why was it significant?

Progress Report 11
1. What was Charlie beginning to realize about Alice Kinnian?
2. What did Charlie find confusing about his dreams and memories?
3. What did Charlie realize from his nightmare about the bloody knife and the free association he did after the dream?
4. Describe the problem Charlie discovered at the bakery, and what he did about it.
5. What did Charlie realize when he talked to Alice about the problem at the bakery?
6. What did Charlie discover in his conversations with various professors and specialists?
7. Describe Charlie's evening out with Alice.
8. What was the status of Charlie's job at the bakery, and what did Charlie conclude because of it?
9. What was Alice's comment when Charlie next visited her?
10. What memory did Charlie experience while he was talking to Alice?

*Flowers For Algernon* Study Questions Page 2

Progress Reports 12-13
1. What was happening to the relationship between Charlie and Drs. Nemur and Strauss?
2. What was happening to Charlie's powers of recall, and what did Charlie think about it?
3. Describe the event involving his sister that Charlie remembered. What was Charlie's feeling upon remembering it?
4. Why did Charlie and Alice have a quarrel?
5. What was Charlie's IQ at this point in the story?
6. Describe the incident in Central Park.
7. What memory was triggered by fastening the seat belt in the airplane?
8. What was Charlie's observation about Dr. Guarino?
9. What was Charlie's main resentment concerning Professor Nemur?
10. Describe the main events at the conference.

Progress Report 14
1. What did Charlie discover when he read the newspaper account of his actions at the conference?
2. What memories did the newspaper article trigger?
3. What did Charlie do when he was in back New York, and why?
4. Describe Charlie's meeting with Fay Lillman, and his observations about her.
5. Describe Charlie's visit to Matt Gordon's barber shop.
6. What gift did Fay bring for Algernon, and why?
7. Describe the first night Charlie spent with Fay.
8. What insights did Charlie share with Alice when he finally contacted her?
9. How did the intelligent Charlie try to distract the child Charlie so the adult could make love to Alice, and was it successful?
10. What did Charlie do when he went back to his apartment?
11. How did Charlie spend the next few weeks?
12. What was Algernon's condition like at this point in the novel?

Progress Reports 15-16
1. Describe Charlie's reception when he takes Algernon back to the lab.
2. What question did Charlie ask Burt, and what was Burt's reply?
3. Where did Charlie want to go, and why?
4. What was Algernon's condition at this point in the novel?
5. Describe the meeting between Alice and Fay.
6. What was Charlie's behavior like after his talk with Alice?
7. What happened at Mrs. Nemur's cocktail party?
8. What did Dr. Strauss say had come up in recent therapy sessions?
9. What was the Algernon-Gordon effect, and what did it mean?

*Flowers For Algernon* Study Questions Page 3

10. What happened to Algernon?
11. Describe Charlie's visit to his mother.
12. Describe Charlie's meeting with Norma.

Progress Report 17
1. Describe Charlie's therapy session with Strauss.
2. What was the first thing Charlie now refused to do for the doctors?
3. What happened when Charlie took the Rorschach test?
4. Describe Alice and Charlie's relationship.
5. What was happening to Charlie, and how was he feeling?
6. What happened when Charlie went back to the bakery?
7. What "Charlie Gordon" did Charlie pull, and what was the result?
8. What was Charlie's plan?
9. What was Charlie's last request in his progress report?
10. What was the length of time that elapsed from the first to the last progress report?

# ANSWER KEY: SHORT ANSWER STUDY QUESTIONS - *Flowers For Algernon*

Progress Reports 1-8

1. How is the novel written?
   It is written in the first person, in the form of progress reports that are given to the doctors.

2. Describe the main character.
   The main character is Charlie Gordon. He is 32 yeas old, and is medically considered a moron, with an IQ of 68. He attends classes at the Beekman College Center for Retarded Adults.

3. What kind of test did Burt give Charlie, and what was the result?
   Burt gave Charlie an inkblot test, which Charlie called the raw shok (actually Rorschach). Charlie was asked to find pictures in the inkblots, but he was not able to do so.

4. Why was Charlie taking the tests?
   He hoped the doctors at Beekman College would use him in an experiment designed to make him smarter.

5. What did Miss Kinnian, Charlie's teacher, tell the doctors about him?
   She said Charlie was her best student, that he wanted to learn to read and write even more than some people who were smarter than he was.

6. What happened when Charlie was given the Thematic Apperception Test?
   He was not able to make up stories about the people in the pictures. He thought it was like telling lies about people he didn't know.

7. Who was Algernon? Describe Charlie's first meeting with him.
   Algernon was a mouse who was given the operation before it was performed on a human. Charlie watched Algernon run the maze, and then Charlie raced against him. They raced ten times and Algernon won all ten races.

8. What was Professor Nemur worried about with regard to the operation?
   He was worried that Charlie would get too intelligent and then get sick from it. He told Charlie that the operation might succeed temporarily, and then leave him worse off than he was before. In that case, Charlie would have to be returned to the Warren State Home.

9. Why did Charlie want to be smart?
   He said that if he were smart he would have friends to talk to and he would never get lonely from talking to himself.

10. What was Mr. Donner's relationship with Charlie?
    Mr. Donner was a friend of Charlie's Uncle Herman. Before he died, Uncle Herman had asked Mr. Donner to watch out for Charlie. Mr. Donner had given Charlie a job at his bakery, and had Charlie released from the Warren Home on a work permit.

11. How did Charlie feel after the operation, and how did the doctors help him?
    He felt discouraged, because he did not see that he was getting any smarter. Dr. Strauss and Professor Nemur gave him a teaching machine to use while he slept. They were very encouraging, telling Charlie that it would take time for the effects of the surgery to begin to show.

12. How long after the surgery was it when Charlie began to see results, and what were they?
    Charlie had the surgery on March 11. In his progress report on March 26, he said he had started dreaming and remembering. Then, on March 29 he beat Algernon. On March 31 he says he is beginning to spell better.

Progress Reports 9-10
1. Describe what happened at the bakery on April Fool's Day.
    The other bakery workers thought they would play an April Fool's joke on Charlie, and Joe Carp told him to work the dough mixer. (Charlie had not been able to do this before.) Charlie worked the mixer correctly, and faster than Oliver, the regular operator. When Mr. Donner found out, he made Charlie the mixer operator and gave him a raise.

2. What did Charlie discover at the party he went to with Joe and Frank?
    He realized that they were making fun of him. After the party, he dreamed about the woman, Ellen.

3. How did Charlie know he was getting smarter?
    He was able to spell correctly and use punctuation. He read quickly, and understood what he was reading. He was beginning to remember things, and the memories appeared like clear pictures.

4. To whom did Charlie talk about his memories and dreams, and why?
    He talked to Dr. Strauss during his twice weekly therapy sessions. Dr. Strauss was a psychiatrist and a neurosurgeon. He told Charlie that his intellectual growth was advancing more rapidly than his emotional growth, and it could cause him problems.

5. Describe what happened when Burt administered the Rorschach test to Charlie.
    Charlie thought he was receiving different instructions this time as compared with the first time he took the test. He thought Burt and Professor Nemur were making fun of him. They

replayed the tape of the first administration and he realized that Burt's wording was the same, but he had given childish answers. He also realized he had reached a new level, and he reacted with anger and suspicion.

6. How were Mr. Donner and the other employees at the bakery reacting to Charlie?
Charlie found a way to speed up production, so Mr. Donner gave him a raise and a bonus. Mr. Donner was also arranging for Charlie to join the baker's union. The other workers seemed afraid of Charlie, and were acting hostile.

7. What was Charlie's IQ at this point in the story?
It was about 100, which is in the normal range.

8. What happened when Charlie overheard Nemur and Strauss discussing the presentation of their findings?
Charlie overheard them arguing about whether or not to report interim findings. He realized that now that he was able to understand what they were talking about, they would object to him listening to their conversation.

9. What concerned Charlie about making friends with some of the boys at the Campus Bowl?
They were discussing the existence of God. This frightened Charlie, because he had just begun to think about what God meant.

10. Describe Charlie's dream about P.S. 13. Why was it significant?
P.S. 13 was the first school Charlie attended. The principal was suggesting to Mrs. Gordon that Charlie attend a special school. Rose was screaming, and insisting that Charlie was normal, and should not go to a special school. Charlie was terrified of the outburst, and had to use the bathroom. Rose refused to take him. She said he was old enough to go by himself. Charlie was not able to control himself, and went to the bathroom in his pants. The dream was significant because Charlie could recall the voices but not see the faces clearly. Also, it was the first time that he remembered his parents' names.

Progress Report 11
1. What was Charlie beginning to realize about Alice Kinnian?
He was becoming attracted to her as a woman, and it confused him.

2. What did Charlie find confusing about his dreams and memories?
He wasn't sure whether they really happened the way he now remembered, or whether he was remembering the way things seemed to be at that time, or if he was inventing the dreams and memories.

3. What did Charlie realize from his nightmare about the bloody knife and the free association he did after the dream?
   He realized that he was not ready to think of a woman romantically or sexually. He also realized he was a person before the surgery, and he wanted to love someone.

4. Describe the problem Charlie discovered at the bakery, and what he did about it.
   He found out that Gimpy was undercharging certain customers, then splitting the difference with them. Professor Nemur told Charlie he was just an innocent bystander, and should not get involved. Dr. Strauss said Charlie was morally obligated to tell Mr. Donner. Alice advised him to make his own decision. He approached Gimpy with a story about a friend who had the problem, and suggested that if the cheating stopped, the friend would not have anything to tell. Gimpy reluctantly agreed, and the cheating stopped.

5. What did Charlie realize when he talked to Alice about the problem at the bakery?
   He realized he was in love with Alice.

6. What did Charlie discover in his conversations with various professors and specialists?
   He discovered that they didn't know much outside of their own specializations, and he was not able to converse with them at the level he had hoped for. He observed that they were not intellectual giants after all, but were only people who were afraid the rest of the world would find out their limitations.

7. Describe Charlie's evening out with Alice.
   They went to an outdoor concert. As Charlie was beginning to get physically close to her, he began to experience physical symptoms of panic. He thought he saw a teenage boy watching them. He realized that he was still an emotional adolescent.

8. What was the status of Charlie's job at the bakery, and what did Charlie conclude because of it?
   Mr. Donner fired him at the request of the other employees. They didn't like his new intelligence and manner. Fanny suspected that he had made a pact with the devil. Charlie realized that his intelligence had driven a wedge between himself and the people he had considered his friends. He wondered what would happen to Algernon if he were put back in a cage with the other mice.

9. What was Alice's comment when Charlie next visited her?
   She told him not to take his firing so hard. The firing had become a symbolic repetition of previous rejections. She said the panic he was feeling was to be expected because he was moving into unknown territory.

10. What memory did Charlie experience while he was talking to Alice?
   He saw his mother with a belt in her hand, screaming at him for looking at a woman. He eventually cried himself to sleep in Alice's arms.

## Progress Reports 12-13

1. What was happening to the relationship between Charlie and Drs. Nemur and Strauss?
   It was becoming strained. Charlie didn't want to turn in progress reports. He resented Nemur referring to him as a laboratory specimen. Strauss reminded Charlie that he needed to write and speak so that others could understand him.

2. What was happening to Charlie's powers of recall, and what did Charlie think about it?
   They were becoming very clear, and were developing rapidly. He thought he would eventually be able to bring his recall completely under his control.

3. Describe the event involving his sister that Charlie remembered. What was Charlie's feeling upon remembering it?
   Norma wanted a dog because she had received an A on a test. Rose had promised she could have one if she got the A. During the family discussion, Norma was mean to Charlie. Matt refused to let her have a dog. Norma then threatened to act like Charlie and not remember anything. After that incident, Norma ignored Charlie, and told her friends he was not her real brother. When he remembered the incident, Charlie felt bad that she had not been able to get the dog.

4. Why did Charlie and Alice have a quarrel?
   Charlie visited the school one night, unannounced. It caused a stir with the other students. After the students left, Alice told him that his attitude toward people had changed, that he was no longer warm and open. She went on to say that she felt inferior to him, and he was getting impatient with her and shutting her out of his life. Then she told him she would not go to the convention with him.

5. What was Charlie's IQ at this point in the story?
   It was 185.

6. Describe the incident in Central Park.
   Charlie met a woman who was making advances toward him. When he discovered she was pregnant, he was repulsed, and started yelling at her. She began screaming and he ran away as others came to help the woman. He was reminded of the way his mother looked before she gave birth to Norma. He was scared because he felt that he wanted the people who helped the woman to catch him and beat him.

7. What memory was triggered by fastening the seat belt in the airplane?
   Charlie remembered going to Dr. Guarino's office for treatments to make him smarter. He remembered being strapped on a table, and hearing his parents argue about the good of the treatment and the money it was costing.

8. What was Charlie's observation about Dr. Guarino?
   He said that even though the treatments didn't work, Guarino had always treated him like a human being.

9. What was Charlie's main resentment concerning Professor Nemur?
   Charlie resented Nemur's constant references to having made Charlie what he was, of referring to him as less than a human being. Nemur did not recognize that Charlie was a human being even before the surgery.

10. Describe the main events at the conference.
    Charlie challenged some of Nemur's conclusions in front of Nemur's colleagues, which greatly embarrassed Nemur. Strauss reminded Charlie that not everyone had his store of knowledge or capability for languages. During the presentations, Charlie's anger increased. He finally released Algernon from his cage, which caused a great commotion. Unknown to the others, he found Algernon and took him back to New York.

Progress Report 14

1. What did Charlie discover when he read the newspaper account of his actions at the conference?
   He read an interview with his sister. He discovered she and his parents were alive. He also read Norma's address in Brooklyn, and found that his father owned a barber shop in the Bronx.

2. What memories did the newspaper article trigger?
   Charlie remembered seeing his sister as a baby. He remembered how his mother's attitude toward him changed as she realized that Norma was normal. He remembered hearing a quarrel between his parents. Rose wanted to put Charlie in a home to protect Norma from possible dangers. Matt disagreed.

3. What did Charlie do when he was in back New York, and why?
   He rented a furnished apartment for himself and Algernon, right near Times Square. He wanted time to rediscover his past and find out more about himself.

4. Describe Charlie's meeting with Fay Lillman, and his observations about her.
    She was his neighbor across the hall. He met her when he asked to use her fire escape to get into his apartment. She was an artist, very messy, and a free spirit. He thought she was attractive and full of life and excitement.

5. Describe Charlie's visit to Matt Gordon's barber shop.
    Charlie let Matt give him a haircut and a shave, all the while wondering if Matt would recognize him. Charlie had a flashback to the night Matt took him to live with Uncle Herman. When it was apparent that Matt didn't recognize him, Charlie left without revealing himself.

6. What gift did Fay bring for Algernon, and why?
    She brought him a female mouse named Minnie. She said he needed female company.

7. Describe the first night Charlie spent with Fay.
    She told him she would go to bed with him. He put her off by saying he wasn't feeling well. Fay got him drunk. In the morning she told him he had talked about wanting to be smart. He also said he couldn't be with her because his mother would take away his peanuts and put him in a cage.

8. What insights did Charlie share with Alice when he finally contacted her?
    He said he realized it was not his intelligence that was coming between them, but his emotional state. He was still reacting to her as the child Charlie who was afraid of women because of the things his mother had done to him.

9. How did the intelligent Charlie try to distract the child Charlie so the adult could make love to Alice, and was it successful?
    The adult Charlie tried to pretend Alice was really Fay. It didn't work-he was able to sit in the dark with Alice, and caress her, but that was all.

10. What did Charlie do when he went back to his apartment?
    He got a bottle of liquor and went over to Fay's apartment. He made love to her.

11. How did Charlie spend the next few weeks?
    He spent most of his time with Fay, dancing, drinking, and making love.

12. What was Algernon's condition like at this point in the novel?
    He was listless and confused, and had a sense of urgency when running the mazes. He injured Minnie, and bit Fay.

Progress Reports 15-16

1. Describe Charlie's reception when he takes Algernon back to the lab.
    The doctors were eager to get Algernon back. Nemur was not happy that Charlie had gone over his head to get a grant from the foundation, but did offer the staff and the lab's resources to help him.

2. What question did Charlie ask Burt, and what was Burt's reply?
    Charlie wanted to know what would happen to him if he regressed. Burt replied that Charlie would be placed in the Warren State Home and Training School. The foundation would pay for his care.

3. Where did Charlie want to go, and why?
    He wanted to visit the Warren School before he regressed and was sent there.

4. What was Algernon's condition at this point in the novel?
    He had stopped running the maze completely. Burt had to force feed him.

5. Describe the meeting between Alice and Fay.
    Fay came into Charlie's apartment while he and Alice were talking. The three of them talked all night. Alice said she liked Fay, but she didn't like to see Charlie drinking and being distracted from his work.

6. What was Charlie's behavior like after his talk with Alice?
    He moved a cot into the lab so he could work around the clock. He wanted to find out what was happening to himself.

7. What happened at Mrs. Nemur's cocktail party?
    Charlie got drunk, and was rude to the other guests. Nemur, Strauss, and Burt became very angry with him. They accused him of endangering their work. Charlie accused them of not caring about him as a person.

8. What did Dr. Strauss say had come up in recent therapy sessions?
    He told the others about Charlie's experiences perceiving himself as he was before the experiment, a separate and distinct individual in the adult Charlie's consciousness.

9. What was the Algernon-Gordon effect, and what did it mean?
    "Artificially induced intelligence deteriorates at a rate of time directly proportional to the quantity of the increase." It meant that Charlie and Algernon would regress mentally.

10. What happened to Algernon?
    He died. Charlie buried him in the back yard and put wild flowers on his grave.

11. Describe Charlie's visit to his mother.
    Rose was not in total command of her mental faculties. She eventually recognized him, but kept forgetting it. She would start raving at the child Charlie, then come back to reality and talk to the adult Charlie.

12. Describe Charlie's meeting with Norma.
    Norma recognized him and was glad to see him. Charlie told her about his memory of the time she wanted a dog, but Norma didn't remember it at all. She told Charlie her mother had told her long ago that Charlie had died in the Warren School. Norma wanted Charlie to take care of her and their mother.

Progress Report 17

1. Describe Charlie's therapy session with Strauss.
   He got lightheaded, and said he felt numb. He had a sensation of expanding up and out, then being pulled back into himself. He felt as if he were shrinking. He saw himself in a cave, and saw a light at the mouth of it, but he couldn't get through the opening.

2. What was the first thing Charlie now refused to do for the doctors?
   He wouldn't do any more mazes.

3. What happened when Charlie took the Rorschach test?
   He told Burt it would be invalid now that he understood the kinds of responses he was supposed to make. Then he forgot what the responses were. He became frustrated and refused to take any more tests.

4. Describe Alice and Charlie's relationship.
   Alice came to visit Charlie. He was able to make love to her. Alice stayed with him for about ten days.

5. What was happening to Charlie, and how was he feeling?
   He was regressing, and he was scared. He wouldn't let anyone else in his apartment.

6. What happened when Charlie went back to the bakery?
   Mr. Donner gave him back his job. A new man began harassing him, and Joe Carp rescued him.

7. What "Charlie Gordon" did Charlie pull, and what was the result?
   He went to Alice's class at the adult center, because he thought he belonged there. His appearance upset her greatly, and she left the room. He suddenly remembered about the operation, and left before she came back.

8. What was Charlie's plan?
   He was going to admit himself to the Warren School so that no one would feel sorry for him.

9. What was Charlie's last request in his progress report?
   He asked that someone put flowers on Algernon's grave.

10. What was the length of time that elapsed from the first to the last progress report?
    The first report was on March 3, and the last one was on November 21. The total length of time was seven months.

MULTIPLE CHOICE STUDY/QUIZ QUESTIONS *Flowers For Algernon*

Progress Reports 1-8

1. True or False: The novel is written in the first person, in the form of progress reports that are given to the doctors.
    A. True
    B. False

2. Which of the following does **not** describe the main character?
    A. His name is Charlie Gordon.
    B. He is medically considered a moron, with an IQ of 68.
    C. He is 25 yeas old.
    D. He attends classes at the Beekman College Center for Retarded Adults.

3. What kind of test did Burt give Charlie, and what was the result?
    A. Burt gave Charlie the Weschler Intelligence Scale for Adults. Charlie got the lowest possible score.
    B. Burt gave Charlie an inkblot test, which Charlie called the raw shok (actually Rorschach.) Charlie was asked to find pictures in the inkblots, but he was not able to do so.
    C. Burt gave Charlie a reading test. He scored a first grade reading level.
    D. Burt gave Charlie a motor coordination test. Charlie scored like a five year old.

4. Why was Charlie taking the tests?
    A. He was applying for a permit to live alone without a guardian.
    B. He wanted to be admitted to a special training school and needed to
    C. He hoped the doctors would use him in an experiment to make him smarter.
    D. He wanted to graduate from the adult school.

5. Who said Charlie wanted to learn to read and write even more than some people who were smarter than he was?
    A. Miss Kinnian
    B. Professor Nemur
    C. Mr. Donner
    D. Charlie

6. Was Charlie able to make up stories about the people in the pictures in the Thematic Apperception Test?
    A. Yes. He had a very vivid imagination.
    B. No. He thought it was like telling lies about people he didn't know.

7. Who was Algernon?
    A. He was the doctor who had devised the surgical procedure.
    B. He was the other person being used in the experiment.
    C. He was a student who was helping with the testing.
    D. He was a mouse who had already had the operation.

8. True or False: Professor Nemur worried that Charlie would keep getting smarter and smarter, until no one in the world could understand him.
    A. True
    B. False

9. Why did Charlie want to be smart?
    A. He wanted to find his parents and take care of them.
    B. He wanted to make enough money to buy things he wanted.
    C. He thought he would have more friends if he were smart.
    D. He wanted to be like his sister.

10. Who was the friend of Charlie's uncle who watched out for Charlie?
    A. It was Herman Gordon.
    B. It was Joe Carp.
    C. It was Burt Selden.
    D. It was Mr. Donner.

11. True or False: After the operation, Charlie felt discouraged, because he did not see that he was getting any smarter.
    A. True
    B. False

12. Which of the following was **not** one of the results Charlie saw within a few weeks after the surgery?
    A. He started dreaming and remembering.
    B. He beat Algernon at the maze.
    C. He started spelling better.
    D. He learned to ride a bike and roller skate.

*Flowers For Algernon* Multiple Choice Questions

Progress Reports 9-10
1. What happened when Joe Carp told Charlie to work the dough mixer?
    A. Charlie broke the mixer and had to pay for repairs out of his salary.
    B. Charlie worked the mixer correctly, and faster than Oliver, the regular operator.
    C. Charlie refused to do it and Joe beat him up.
    D. Charlie tried, but dough came pouring out all over the floor.

2. What did Charlie discover at the party he went to with Joe and Frank?
    A. He thought he was falling in love with Ellen.
    B. He discovered he liked to drink beer.
    C. He found out he was a good dancer.
    D. He realized that they were making fun of him.

3. How did Charlie's memories seem to him?
    A. The memories appeared like clear pictures.
    B. They were like paintings in a museum.
    C. They were blurry and confusing.
    D. They seemed like they had happened to someone else.

4. To whom did Charlie talk about his memories and dreams?
    A. He talked to Algernon.
    B. He talked to Mr. Donner.
    C. He talked to Dr. Strauss.
    D. He talked to Burt Selden.

5. Describe what happened when Burt administered the Rorschach test to Charlie.
    A. He said it was easier than the first time he took it.
    B. He refused to take it.
    C. He said Burt was administering it incorrectly.
    D. He thought he was receiving different instructions than the first time.

6. True or False: The other workers at the bakery were friendlier since they saw that Charlie was smarter.
    A. True
    B. False

7. What was Charlie's IQ at this point in the story?
   A. It was about 100.
   B. It was 133.
   C. It was 250.
   D. It was 82.

8. True or False: Charlie overheard Nemur and Strauss arguing about whether or not to report interim findings. He realized that now that he was able to understand what they were talking about, they would object to him listening to their conversation.
   A. True
   B. False

9. What concerned Charlie about making friends with some of the boys at the Campus Bowl?
   A. They were talking about girls. He was still afraid of girls and didn't want them to know it.
   B. They were discussing the existence of God. This frightened Charlie, because he had just begun to think about what God meant.
   C. He was afraid they would find out he didn't go to college.
   D. He thought he was too old to become friends with any of them.

10. Why was Charlie's dream about P.S. 13 significant?
    A. It was his first dream in a foreign language.
    B. He was able to see clearly but not hear anything.
    C. It was the first time that he remembered his parents' names.
    D. Everyone in it looked like him.

*Flowers For Algernon* Multiple Choice Questions

Progress Report 11

1. True or False: Charlie was becoming attracted to Alice Kinnian as a woman, and it confused him.
    A. True
    B. False

2. What did Charlie find confusing about his dreams and memories?
    A. He didn't remember some of the people in them.
    B. He didn't know whether or not to talk about them.
    C. He wasn't sure whether they really happened the way he now remembered.
    D. They made him upset, and he never used to get upset.

3. What did Charlie realize from his nightmare about the bloody knife and the free association he did after the dream?
    A. He realized he was a person before the surgery, and he wanted to love someone.
    B. He realized he must have been attacked by someone with a knife.
    C. He realized he was reliving the surgery.
    D. He realized he had suicidal tendencies.

4. What problem did Charlie discover at the bakery?
    A. Gimpy was cheating Mr. Donner.
    B. Mr. Donner was having an affair with one of the customers.
    C. Joe was putting spoiled ingredients in some of the pastries.
    D. The store had been cited for being unsanitary.

5. What did Charlie realize when he talked to Alice about the problem at the bakery?
    A. He realized he had a conscience.
    B. He realized he was in love with Alice.
    C. He realized he didn't like the people at the bakery.
    D. He realized he didn't like being smart.

6. True or False: Charlie discovered that the various professors and specialists he talked to didn't know much outside of their own specializations, and he was not able to converse with them at the level he had hoped for.
    A. True
    B. False

7. Which of the following did **not** happen during Charlie's evening out with Alice?
    A. They went to an outdoor concert.
    B. Alice told Charlie she wanted to have a physical relationship with him.
    C. Charlie began to experience physical symptoms of panic.
    D. Charlie realized that he was still an emotional adolescent.

8. What was the status of Charlie's job at the bakery?
    A. He was promoted to manager.
    B. He left because it was not challenging any more.
    C. He told Mr. Donner he only wanted to do the jobs he used to do.
    D. Mr. Donner fired him at the request of the other employees.

9. Who told Charlie that the panic he was feeling was to be expected because he was moving into unknown territory?
    A. Alice
    B. Professor Nemur
    C. Burt
    D. Mr. Donner

10. What memory did Charlie experience while he was talking to Alice?
    A. He remembered the first time he ever felt stupid.
    B. He saw a group of children laughing at him when he could not catch a football.
    C. He remembered his father trying to teach him to ride a bike, but he kept falling off.
    D. He saw his mother with a belt in her hand, screaming at him for looking at a woman.

*Flowers For Algernon* Multiple Choice Questions

Progress Reports 12-13

1. True or False: Doctors Nemur and Strauss were beginning to treat Charlie like an equal, and ask his opinion about their experiments.
    A. True
    B. False

2. What was happening to Charlie's powers of recall?
    A. They were becoming slower and less reliable.
    B. They were becoming very clear, and were developing rapidly.
    C. He could only recall events that happened a long time ago.
    D. He could recall events, but he could not recognize people.

3. Describe the event involving his sister that Charlie remembered.
    A. Norma wanted to have a pajama party but her mother would not let her. She was afraid Charlie would hurt the other girls.
    B. Norma tried teaching Charlie to swim, and he almost drowned.
    C. Norma wanted a dog, but Matt refused. After that, Norma ignored Charlie, and told her friends he was not her real brother.
    D. Charlie picked Norma up out of her crib and dropped her on the floor. His mother beat him and locked him in his room.

4. True or False: Alice told Charlie that his attitude toward people had changed, that he was no longer warm and open. She went on to say that she felt inferior to him, and he was getting impatient with her and shutting her out of his life.
    A. True
    B. False

5. What was Charlie's IQ at this point in the story?
    A. It was 112.
    B. It was 263.
    C. It was 156.
    D. It was 185.

6. What scared Charlie about the incident in Central Park?
    A. He had never seen a pregnant woman.
    B. He was afraid he would be picked up by the police for loitering in the park.
    C. He wanted the people who helped the woman to catch him and beat him.
    D. He was afraid if Alice found out she would stop speaking to him.

7. What memory was triggered by fastening the seat belt in the airplane?
   A. He remembered going to Dr. Guarino's office.
   B. He remembered his mother tying him to a chair.
   C. He remembered being strapped down for the surgery.
   D. He remembered his father taking him for rides in his stroller.

8. What was Charlie's observation about Dr. Guarino?
   A. Guarino was a quack.
   B. Guarino had molested him and made him promise not to tell.
   C. Guarino meant well, but was not very bright.
   D. Guarino had treated him as a human being.

9. Whom did Charlie resent for not recognizing that Charlie was a human being even before the surgery?
   A. Alice
   B. Dr. Strauss
   C. Professor Nemur
   D. Mr. Donner

10. What did Charlie do at the conference?
    A. He supported Nemur's conclusions in front of Nemur's colleagues.
    B. He released Algernon from his cage, and took him back to New York.
    C. He went berserk and started dancing on the conference table.
    D. He refused to talk to anyone about his life before or after the surgery.

*Flowers For Algernon*

Progress Report 14

1. What did Charlie discover when he read the newspaper account of his actions at the conference?
    A. He discovered his mother was dead.
    B. He found out there was a reward being offered for information about him.
    C. He discovered that a television producer wanted to make a movie about him.
    D. He read Norma's address in Brooklyn.

2. What memories did the newspaper article trigger?
    A. He remembered how his mother's attitude toward him changed as she realized that Norma was normal.
    B. He remembered Matt taking him to the Warren School and leaving him there.
    C. He remembered Norma crying because he broke her doll.
    D. He remembered feeling unloved and unwanted.

3. What did Charlie do when he was back in New York?
    A. He applied for graduate school at Columbia University.
    B. He contacted the newspaper and offered them and interview.
    C. He rented a furnished apartment for himself and Algernon.
    D. He went to see three Broadway plays every day for a week.

4. Describe Charlie's observations about Fay Lillman.
    A. He thought she was morally corrupt.
    B. He thought she was attractive and full of life and excitement.
    C. He thought she was boring and dull.
    D. He thought she was the perfect woman for him.

5. Did Charlie reveal himself to his father at the barber shop?
    A. Yes
    B. No

6. What gift did Fay bring for Algernon?
    A. She brought him a block of sharp cheddar cheese.
    B. She brought him one of her paintings.
    C. She brought him a stuffed cat to play with.
    D. She brought him a female mouse named Minnie.

7. True or False: On the first night they spent together, Charlie told Fay he couldn't play with her because his mother would take away his peanuts and put him in a cage.
    A. True
    B. False

8. What insights did Charlie share with Alice when he finally contacted her?
    A. He said he realized his emotional state was coming between them.
    B. He said he realized his intellectual state was coming between them.
    C. He said he did not have time for women; he had to devote himself to work.
    D. He said he really loved Fay.

9. How did the intelligent Charlie try to distract the child Charlie so the adult could make love to Alice?
    A. The intelligent Charlie got drunk.
    B. The intelligent Charlie had Dr. Strauss hypnotize him.
    C. The intelligent Charlie thought about his fondest memories while with Alice.
    D. The intelligent Charlie tried to pretend Alice was really Fay.

10. What did Charlie do when he went back to his apartment?
    A. He spent a few hours setting up new mazes for Algernon, then went to bed.
    B. He wrote a long progress report, then burned it.
    C. He got a bottle of liquor and went over to Fay's apartment. He made love to her.
    D. He went out for a walk around Times Square.

11. How did Charlie spend the next few weeks?
    A. He traveled around the country to speak with scientists and doctors.
    B. He stayed in the apartment with Algernon.
    C. He spent most of his time with Fay, dancing, drinking, and making love.
    D. He wrote a book about his experiences.

12. Which of the following does not describe Algernon's condition at this point in the novel?
    A. He was listless and confused
    B. He was protective of Minnie.
    C. He had a sense of urgency when running the mazes.
    D. He bit Fay.

*Flowers For Algernon* Multiple Choice Questions

Progress Reports 15-16

1. True or False: Nemur was not happy that Charlie had gone over his head to get a grant from the foundation, but did offer the staff and the lab's resources to help him.
   A. True
   B. False

2. Charlie wanted to know what would happen to him if he regressed. What was Burt's reply?
   A. Alice had offered to take care of him.
   B. He would be sent to live with his sister.
   C. Charlie would be placed in the Warren State Home and Training School.
   D. He would be kept in a special room in the lab for further research.

3. Where did Charlie want to go?
   A. He wanted to see his old house.
   B. He wanted to visit the Warren School.
   C. He wanted to take Alice on a vacation.
   D. He wanted to go dancing and drinking again with Fay.

4. What was Algernon's condition at this point in the novel?
   A. He had improved his performance in the mazes.
   B. He was the same as he was before.
   C. He would only respond to Charlie.
   D. He had stopped running he maze completely. Burt had to force feed him.

5. True or False: Alice told Charlie that Fay was a vile, stupid whore.
   A. True
   B. False

6. What was Charlie's behavior like after his talk with Alice?
   A. He became withdrawn and unresponsive.
   B. He stayed out all night partying with Fay to forget about his problems.
   C. He moved a cot into the lab so he could work around the clock.
   D. He was kinder and more cooperative with everyone.

7. What happened at Mrs. Nemur's cocktail party?
   A. Charlie made a pass at Mrs. Nemur.
   B. Charlie impressed Mr. Raynor and got another grant.
   C. Charlie got drunk, and was rude to the other guests.
   D. Charlie had a panic attack and hid in the bathroom most of the evening.

8. True or False: Charlie had been perceiving himself as he was before the experiment, a separate and distinct individual in the adult Charlie's consciousness.
    A. True
    B. False

9. What was the name of the following theory? "Artificially induced intelligence deteriorates at a rate of time directly proportional to the quantity of the increase."
    A. the Strauss Syndrome
    B. Nemur's Neurological Hypothesis
    C. the Beekman Theory of Intelligence
    D. the Algernon-Gordon Effect

10. True or False: When Algernon died, Charlie had him cremated. He put Algernon's ashes on a shelf in his apartment, and kept a bouquet of fresh flowers there.
    A. True
    B. False

11. Which of the following describes Charlie's visit to his mother?
    A. Rose was not in total command of her mental faculties. She would start raving at the child Charlie, then come back to reality and talk to the adult Charlie.
    B. Rose told him her son was dead. She refused to let him in. He left without talking to her.
    C. Rose was glad to see him. They talked for a long time. She explained her fears and feelings from when he was small. They parted on good terms.
    D. Rose refused to believe he got smarter. She thought it was an impostor playing a trick on her. Charlie could not convince her to believe otherwise.

12. True or False: Norma still remembered the incident about the dog. She told Charlie she would never forgive him.
    A. True
    B. False

*Flowers For Algernon* Multiple Choice Questions

Progress Report 17
1.  Which of the following did not happen during Charlie's therapy session with Strauss?
    A. He got lightheaded, and said he felt numb.
    B. He had a sensation of expanding up and out, then being pulled back into himself. C. He felt as if he were on fire.
    D. He saw himself in a cave, but he couldn't get through the opening.

2.  What was the first thing Charlie now refused to do for the doctors?
    A. He wouldn't write progress reports.
    B. He wouldn't do any more mazes.
    C. He would not look at them.
    D. He would not tell them what he was thinking or feeling.

3.  What happened when Charlie took the Rorschach test?
    A. He got all of the answers correct.
    B. He got angry and ripped up the cards.
    C. He gave Burt the same answer for every card.
    D. He became frustrated and refused to take any more tests.

4.  Was Charlie able to overcome his panic and make love to Alice?
    A. Yes, he was.
    B. No, he was not.

5.  True or False: Charlie thought he was getting smarter again.
    A. True
    B. False

6.  What happened when Charlie went back to the bakery?
    A. The other men didn't believe he was no longer smart. They sent him away.
    B. He got scared and didn't go in.
    C. Mr. Donner gave him back his job.
    D. He found out Gimpy was running the bakery. Gimpy would not re-hire him.

7.  What "Charlie Gordon" did Charlie pull?
    A. He got lost on the way home and went to his old room instead of his apartment.
    B. He forgot Algernon was dead and went to the lab to visit him.
    C. He climbed in Fay's window and interrupted her while she was with another man.
    D. He went to Alice's class at the adult center.

8. What was Charlie's plan?
   A. He was going to admit himself to the Warren School so that no one would feel sorry for him.
   B. He was going to live with his mother and Norma.
   C. He was going to kill himself.
   D. He was going to continue working at the bakery and living alone.

9. What was Charlie's request in his last progress report?
   A. He asked Professor Nemur to use his (Charlie's) research to find a way to make him smart again.
   B. He asked Alice to visit him and write letters to him.
   C. He asked that someone put flowers on Algernon's grave.
   D. He asked Burt to make sure Norma got the money in his savings account.

10. What was the length of time that elapsed from the first to the last progress report?
    A. three years
    B. fifty-six days
    C. eighteen months
    D. seven months

## ANSWER KEY-MULTIPLE CHOICE QUIZ/STUDY GUIDE QUESTIONS
### *Flowers for Algernon*

| Progress Reports 1-8 | Progress Reports 9-10 | Progress Report 11 |
|---|---|---|
| 1. A True | 1. B | 1. A. True |
| 2. C | 2. D | 2. C |
| 3. B | 3. A | 3. A |
| 4. C | 4. C | 4. A |
| 5. A | 5. D | 5. B |
| 6. B | 6. B False | 6. A True |
| 7. D | 7. A | 7. B |
| 8. B. False | 8. A True | 8. D |
| 9. C | 9. B | 9. C |
| 10. D | 10. C | 10. D |
| 11. A True | | |
| 12. D | | |

| Progress Reports 12-13 | Progress Report 14 | Progress Reports 15-16 |
|---|---|---|
| 1. B False | 1. D | 1. A True |
| 2. B | 2. A | 2. C |
| 3. C | 3. C | 3. B |
| 4. A True | 4. B | 4. D |
| 5. D | 5. B | 5. B |
| 6. C | 6. D | 6. C |
| 7. A | 7. A True | 7. C |
| 8. D | 8. A | 8. A True |
| 9. C | 9. D | 9. D |
| 10. B | 10. C | 10. B False |
| 11. | 11. C | 11. A |
| | 12. B | 12. B False |

Progress Report 17

1. C
2. B
3. D
4. A
5. B False
6. C
7. D
8. A
9. C
10. D

# PREREADING VOCABULARY WORKSHEETS

Vocabulary Progress Reports 1-8

Part I: Using Prior Knowledge and Context Clues
Below are the sentences in which the vocabulary words appear in the text. Read the sentence. Use any clues you can find in the sentence combined with your prior knowledge, and write what you think the underlined words mean on the lines provided.
Note: Some of the vocabulary words are spelled the way Charlie spelled them in his progress reports. When this occurs, also write the correct spelling. Only the correct spelling will be used in tests and other activities.

1. Prof Nemur says if it werks good and its *perminint* they will make other pepul like me smart also.

   _____

2. He says the boy needs the mony Charlie so Im going to keep him on as an *aprentise* to lern him to be a baker.

   _____

3. A bakers werk is very importint and very *complikated* and you shouldnt worry about things like that.

   _____

4. Theres the SUBCONSCIOUS *and the* CONSCIOUS (thats how you spell it) and one dont tell the other what its doing.

   _____

5. Its called Robinson Crusoe about a man who gets *merooned* on a dessert iland.

   _____

Part II: Determining the Meaning   Match the vocabulary words to their dictionary definitions.

   1. permanent         A. one who is learning a trade or occupation
   2. apprentice        B. isolated with little help of rescue
   3. complicated       C. waking awareness perceptible at any time
   4. conscious         D. not expected to change
   5. marooned          E. not easy to understand or analyze

Vocabulary Progress Reports 9-10

Part I: Using Prior Knowledge and Context Clues
   Below are the sentences in which the vocabulary words appear in the text. Read the sentence. Use any clues you can find in the sentence combined with your prior knowledge, and write what you think the underlined words mean on the lines provided.

1. Frank said I told you there is something *peculier* lately about Charlie.

   _____

2. She said I reached a *plateau.*

   _____

3. "It's a requirement of these tests that the *procedure* be the same each time it's administered."

   _____

4. "It's a requirement of these tests that the procedure be the same each time it's *administered*."

   _____

5. Charlie *hunches* over on his stool, intently watching Gimpy pick up the knife and cut off a slab of dough.

   _____

6. He *cowers*, not knowing what she will do.

   _____

7. His arms go up automatically to *ward* off blows.

   _____

8. Dad *massive* and slumped.

   _____

Vocabulary Progress Reports 9-10 Continued

9. Hearing them now, arguing with each other across the years, I have the *impulse* to shout at them.

_____

Part II: Determining the Meaning  Match the vocabulary words to their dictionary definitions.

1. peculiar
2. plateau
3. procedure
4. administered
5. hunches
6. cowers
7. ward
8. massive
9. impulse

A. cringes in fear
B. a series of steps taken to do something
C. large or imposing
D. unusual or eccentric
E. assumes a crouched or cramped posture
F. given out; dispensed
G. a sudden wish that prompts an act or thought
H. a stable level, period, or state
I. to try to prevent; avert

Vocabulary Progress Report 11

Part I: Using Prior Knowledge and Context Clues

Below are the sentences in which the vocabulary words appear in the text. Read the sentence. Use any clues you can find in the sentence combined with your prior knowledge, and write what you think the underlined words mean on the lines provided.

1. The sudden memory shows him that his hatred is really directed at a *depraved* governess who had terrified him with frightening stories and left a flaw in his personality.

   _____

2. He takes her in his arms and the *implication* is that all his problems have been solved.

   _____

3. The parts have to be *consistent* and belong together.

   _____

4. "You've got *obligations* now-not only to Professor Nemur and Dr. Strauss, but to the millions who may follow in your footsteps."

   _____

5. What's right? *Ironic* that all my intelligence doesn't help me solve a problem like this.

   _____

6. Smug, *pompous*-- I felt like hitting him, too.

   _____

7. I had to trust my *intuition*.

   _____

8. The more I thought about him, the worse became the *queasy* feeling that comes before fainting.

   _____

Vocabulary Progress Report 11 Continued

9. Before, they had laughed at me, *despising* me for my ignorance and dullness; now, they hated me for my knowledge and understanding.

___

10. On the far wall, across from the sofa, hung an *ornately* framed reproduction of Picasso's "Mother and Child."

___

11. "This terror at being kicked out of the bakery is *vague*, a fear I don't understand."

___

Part II: Determining the Meaning   Match the vocabulary words to their dictionary definitions.

1. depraved
2. implication
3. consistent
4. obligations
5. ironic
6. pompous
7. intuition
8. queasy
9. despising
10. ornately
11. vague

A. corrupt, wicked
B. excessive self-esteem or exaggerated dignity
C. duties or promises
D. disliking intensely; loathing
E. knowing or sensing without rational processes
F. indistinctly felt, perceived, or understood
G. causing nausea; sickening
H. done in a flashy or showy manner
I. contrary to what was expected or intended
J. reliable or uniform
K. that which is hinted at or suggested

Vocabulary Progress Reports 12-13

Part I: Using Prior Knowledge and Context Clues

Below are the sentences in which the vocabulary words appear in the text. Read the sentence. Use any clues you can find in the sentence combined with your prior knowledge, and write what you think the underlined words mean on the lines provided.

1. Our relationship remains *platonic*.

   _____

2. "Did you think I'd remain a *docile* pup, wagging my tail and licking the foot that kicks me?"

   _____

3. Standing there with her coat open, she was *superimposed* as a double exposure on the picture of the middle-aged woman just out to the bathtub, holding open her bathrobe for Charlie to see.

   _____

4. A *degenerate* tried to rape her.

   _____

5. "First there will have to be physical and mental tests to determine the causes of the *pathology*."

   _____

6. "There will be enough time later to talk of *prognosis*."

   _____

7. As Burt would put it, mocking the *euphemisms* of educational jargon, I'm exceptional . . . .

   _____

8. It's *paradoxical* that an ordinary man like Nemur presumes to devote himself to making other people geniuses.

   _____

Vocabulary Progress Reports 12-13 Continued

9. I've got to realize that when they continually *admonish* me to speak and write simply so that people who read these reports will be able to understand me, they are talking about themselves as well.

_____

10. When someone from the audience asked Burt if he was suggesting that this *erratic* behavior was directly caused by increased intelligence, Burt ducked the question.

_____

11. The constant *juxtaposition* of "Algernon and Charlie," and "Charlie and Algernon," made it clear that they thought of both of us as a couple of experimental animals who had no existence outside the laboratory.

_____

Part II: Determining the Meaning   Match the vocabulary words to their dictionary definitions.

1. platonic
2. docile
3. superimposed
4. degenerate
5. pathology
6. prognosis
7. euphemisms
8. paradoxical
9. admonish
10. erratic
11. juxtaposition

A. a depraved, corrupt, or vicious person
B. prediction of the course and outcome of a disease
C. seemingly contradictory but possibly true
D. lacking consistency, uniformity, or regularity
E. spiritual and ideal, but not physical
F. to reprove gently but earnestly
G. a deviation from a normal condition
H. placement side by side for comparison
I. yielding to supervision or direction
J. mild terms substituted for offensive ones
K. placed on or over something else

Vocabulary Progress Report 14

Part I: Using Prior Knowledge and Context Clues

Below are the sentences in which the vocabulary words appear in the text. Read the sentence. Use any clues you can find in the sentence combined with your prior knowledge, and write what you think the underlined words mean on the lines provided.

1. The headline read: *Moron-Genius and Mouse Go Berserk.*

   _____

2. Fortunately, as a *precaution*, I withdrew my savings from the bank as soon as I arrived in New York.

   _____

3. I tried to keep my *composure*.

   _____

4. "But you were *phenomenal*. What an act!"

   _____

5. I longed to reach out for her, but I knew it was *futile*. In spite of the operation Charlie was still with me.

   _____

6. I have often reread my early progress reports and seen the illiteracy, the childish *naïveté*, the mind of low intelligences peering from a dark room, through the keyhole, at the dazzling light outside.

   _____

7. "I had horrible visions of you dead in an alleyway, or wandering around skid row with *amnesia*."

   _____

Vocabulary Progress Report 14 Continued

8. "I can't help feeling that I'm not me. I've *usurped* his place and locked him out the way they locked me out of the bakery."

___

9. I can't help but admire the structural linguists who have carved out for themselves a linguistic discipline based on the *deterioration* of written communication.

___

Part II: Determining the Meaning   Match the vocabulary words to their dictionary definitions.

1. berserk                A. destructively or frenetically violent
2. precaution             B. partial or total loss of memory
3. composure              C. extraordinary; outstanding
4. phenomenal             D. the state of being artless or uncritical
5. futile                 E. diminishing in quality
6. naïveté                F. action taken in advance to protect against failure
7. amnesia                G. taken over or occupied without the right to do so
8. usurped                H. a calm or tranquil state of mind
9. deterioration          I. having no useful result

Vocabulary Progress Reports 15-16

Part I: Using Prior Knowledge and Context Clues
　　Below are the sentences in which the vocabulary words appear in the text. Read the sentence. Use any clues you can find in the sentence combined with your prior knowledge, and write what you think the underlined words mean on the lines provided.

1. He was doing his best to be *cordial*, but I could see by his face that he was skeptical.

   _____

2. He was doing his best to be cordial, but I could see by his face that he was *skeptical*.

   _____

3. "I'm sure that from the beginning you planned for all *exigencies*. So what happens to me?"

   _____

4. *Imperceptibly,* I could see her relax.

   _____

5. He has moments out of his *lethargy*. Periodically, he will run a shifting maze, but when he fails and finds himself in a dead-end, he reacts violently.

   _____

6. When I picked him up, he made no attempt to uncurl, but remained in that state much like a catatonic *stupor.*

   _____

7. "I'll admit I'm like him in a number of ways, but humility and self-effacement are not among them. I've learned how little they get a person in this world." "You've become *cynical*," said Nemur.

   _____

8. But my tongue kept getting in the way, like a huge *obstruction*, and my mouth was dry.

   _____

Vocabulary Progress Reports 15-16 Continued

9. But she had gone inside the *vestibule* and locked the door.

___

10. It had never occurred to me that all these years alone with my mother might change her. And yet it was *inevitable*. She was no longer the spoiled brat of my memories.

___

Part II: Determining the Meaning    Match the vocabulary words to their dictionary definitions.

1. cordial
2. skeptical
3. exigencies
4. imperceptibly
5. lethargy
6. stupor
7. cynical
8. obstruction
9. vestibule
10. inevitable

A. impossible to avoid or prevent
B. expressing scorn and bitter mockery
C. not aware of
D. sluggishness, inactivity, and apathy
E. something that gets in the way
F. marked by or given to doubt; questioning
G. a passage between outer door and interior of house
H. urgent requirements
I. warm and sincere; friendly
J. mental numbness

Vocabulary Progress Report 17

Part I: Using Prior Knowledge and Context Clues

    Below are the sentences in which the vocabulary words appear in the text. Read the sentence. Use any clues you can find in the sentence combined with your prior knowledge, and write what you think the underlined words mean on the lines provided.

1. I lay down on the couch immediately, and he, as usual, took his seat to one side and a little behind me- just out of sight- and waited for me to begin the ritual of pouring out all the *accumulated* poisons of the mind.

   _____

2. But now I felt *isolated* and empty.

   _____

3. Small at first, *encompassing* with my body, the room, the building, the city, the country, until I know that if I look down I will see my shadow blotting out the earth.

   _____

4. Slowly, as waves *recede*, my expanding spirit shrinks back into earthly dimensions--not voluntarily, because I would prefer to lose myself, but I am pulled from below, back to myself, into myself, so that for just one moment I am on the couch again, fitting the fingers of my awareness into the glove of my flesh.

   _____

5. I stare inward in the center of my unseeing eye at the red spot that transforms itself into a multipetaled flower-the shimmering, swirling, *luminescent* flower that lies deep in the core of my unconscious.

   _____

6. I open my eyes, blinded by the intense light. And *flail* the air and tremble and scream.

   _____

Vocabulary Progress Report 17 Continued

7. "It's not *valid*," I said. "I know what you're looking for. I know the kind of responses I'm supposed to have, to create a certain picture of what my mind is like."

___

8. I had unwound the string that she had given me, and found my way out of the *labyrinth* to where she was waiting.

___

9. Alice tells me I lie in bed for days and don't seem to know who or where I am. Then it all comes back and I recognize her and remember what's happening. *Fugues* of amnesia.

___

Part II: Determining the Meaning   Match the vocabulary words to their dictionary definitions.

1. accumulated
2. isolated
3. encompassing
4. recede
5. luminescent
6. flail
7. valid
8. labyrinth
9. fugues

A. surrounding
B. to move back or away from a limit
C. a maze
D. to strike or lash out violently
E. amnesiac conditions
F. to set apart or cut off from others
G. producing the desired results
H. emitting light
I. gathered or piled up

## ANSWER KEY-PREREADING VOCABULARY WORKSHEETS
*Flowers for Algernon*

Progress Reports 1-8
1. D
2. A
3. E
4. C
5. B

Progress Reports 9-10
1. D
2. H
3. B
4. F
5. E
6. A
7. I
8. C
9. G

Progress Report 11
1. A
2. K
3. J
4. C
5. I
6. B
7. E
8. G
9. D
10. H
11. F

Progress Reports 12-13
1. E
2. I
3. K
4. A
5. G
6. B
7. J
8. C
9. F
10. D
11. H

Progress Report 14
1. A
2. F
3. H
4. C
5. I
6. D
7. B
8. G
9. E

Progress Reports 15-16
1. I
2. F
3. H
4. C
5. D
6. J
7. B
8. E
9. G
10. A

Progress Report 17
1. I
2. F
3. A
4. B
5. H
6. D
7. G
8. C
9. E

# DAILY LESSON PLANS

# LESSON ONE

Objectives
1. To introduce the *Flowers for Algernon* unit
2. To relate students' prior knowledge to the new material
3. To distribute books and other related materials
4. To do the prereading work for Progress Reports 1-8

Activity #1

Distribute copies of a maze. (Most magazine racks have books of puzzles and mazes.) Have students work with a partner to time each other as they complete the maze. Find the average length of time it took for students to work the maze. Then categorize students as average, below average, and above average. Invite students to discuss how they feel about being labeled on the basis of a test.

Activity #2

Introduce the novel *Flowers for Algernon*. Tell students it is a science fiction novel. Science fiction is defined as literature that has elements of science or technology as a focus of the conflict or setting. It is often concerned with the effects of science and technology on people. Encourage students to look for the scientific and technological elements while they are reading. The main character in the novel is asked to complete mazes like the one the students just did. Ask why someone would be asked to perform such a task.

Activity #3

Ask what students think the title could be referring to. Do a group KWL sheet with the students (form included.) Put any information the students know in the K column (What I Know.) Ask students what they want to find out and put that information in the W column (What I Want to Find Out.) Keep the sheet and refer back to it after reading the novel, and complete the L column (What I Learned.)

Activity #4

Distribute the materials students will use in this unit. Explain in detail how students are to use these materials.

Study Guides  Students should preview the study guide questions before each reading assignment to get a feeling for what events and ideas are important in that section. After reading the section, students will (as a class or individually) answer the questions to review the important events and ideas from that section of the book. Students should keep the study guides as study materials for the unit test.

<u>Reading Assignment Sheet</u>  You need to fill in the reading assignment sheet to let students know when their reading has to be completed. You can either write the assignment sheet on a side blackboard or bulletin board and leave it there for students to see each day, or you can "ditto" copies for each student to have. In either case, you should advise students to become very familiar with the reading assignments so they know what is expected of them.

<u>Extra Activities Center</u>  The Unit Resources portion of this unit contains suggestions for a library of related books and articles in your classroom as well as crossword and word search puzzles. Make an extra activities center in your room where you will keep these materials for students to use. (Bring the books and articles in from the library and keep several copies of the puzzles on hand.) Explain to students that these materials are available for students to use when they finish reading assignments or other class work early.

<u>Books</u>  Each school has its own rules and regulations regarding student use of school books. Advise students of the procedures that are normal for your school.

<u>Activity #5</u>

Show students how to preview the study questions and do the vocabulary work for Progress Reports 1-8 of *Flowers for Algernon*. If students do not finish this assignment in class, they should complete it prior to the next class meeting.

NOTE: Throughout the novel there are descriptions of Charlie's dreams and emerging memories. Read these aloud to students as they close their eyes and try to visualize the dreams.

KWL *Flowers for Algernon*

**Directions:** Before reading, think about what you already know about Daniel Keyes and/or *Flowers for Algernon*. Write the information in the K column. Think about what you would like to find out from reading the book. Write your questions in the W column. After you have read the book, use the L column to write the answers to your questions from the W column, and anything else you remember from the book.

| K - What I Know | W - What I Want To Find Out | L - What I Learned |
|---|---|---|
| | | |

# LESSON TWO

Objectives
1. To read Progress Reports 1-8
2. To review the main ideas and events from Progress Reports 1-8
3. To introduce the Nonfiction assignment

Activity #1

You may want to read Progress Reports 1 and 2 aloud to the students to set the mood for the novel. Invite willing students to read Progress Reports 3-8 aloud to the rest of the class.

Activity #2

Give the students time to answer the study guide questions, and then discuss the answers in detail. Write the answers on the board or overhead projector so students can have the correct answers for study purposes. Encourage students to take notes. If the students own their books, encourage them to use highlighter pens to mark important passages and the answers to the study guide questions.

Note: It is a good practice in public speaking and leadership skills for individual students to take charge of leading the discussion of the study questions. Perhaps a different student could go to the front of the class and lead the discussion each day that the study questions are discussed during this unit. Of course, the teacher should guide the discussion when appropriate and be sure to fill in any gaps the students leave.

Activity #3

Distribute copies of the Nonfiction Assignment sheet and go over it in detail with the students. Give them the due date for the assignment (Lesson 18.) Encourage them to focus on topics that are relevant to the novel. Some possible topics are: Real experiments and programs designed to increase intelligence; the field of intelligence testing; the treatment of mentally handicapped individuals in society; programs to help mildly mentally handicapped adults live outside of institutions; the conditions inside mental institutions; advances in the field of studying mental handicaps; varying opinions on scientific experimentation using animals; school programs for mentally handicapped students.

NONFICTION ASSIGNMENT SHEET *Flowers for Algernon*
(To be completed after reading the required nonfiction article)

Name _____ Date _____ Class _____

Title of Nonfiction Read _____

Written By _____ Publication Date _____

I. Factual Summary: Write a short summary of the piece you read.

II. Vocabulary:
   1. With which vocabulary words in the piece did you encounter some degree of difficulty?

   2. How did you resolve your lack of understanding with these words?

III. Interpretation: What was the main point the author wanted you to get from reading his/her work?

IV. Criticism:
   1. With which points of the piece did you agree or find easy to accept? Why?

   2. With which points of the piece did you disagree or find difficult to believe? Why?

V. Personal Response: What do you think about this piece? OR How does this piece influence your ideas?

## LESSON THREE

Objectives
1. To do the prereading and vocabulary work for Progress Reports 9-10
2. To read Progress Reports 9-10
3. To give students practice reading orally
4. To evaluate students' oral reading

Activity #1

Give students about fifteen minutes to preview the study questions for Progress Reports 9-10 and do the related vocabulary work.

Activity #2

Have students read Progress Reports 9-10 of *Flowers for Algernon* out loud in class. You probably know the best way to get readers with your class; pick students at random, ask for volunteers, or use whatever method works best for your group. If you have not yet completed an oral reading evaluation for your students for this marking period, this would be a good opportunity to do so. A form is included with this unit for your convenience.

If students do not complete reading Progress Reports 9-10 in class, they should do so prior to your next class meeting.

## LESSON FOUR

Objectives
1. To check students' understanding of the main ideas from Progress Reports 1-10
2. To preview the study questions for Progress Report 11
3. To familiarize students with the vocabulary in Progress Report 11
4. To read Progress Report 11

Activity #1

Quiz--distribute quizzes (multiple choice study questions for Progress Reports 1-10) and give students about ten minutes to complete them. Have students exchange papers. Grade the quizzes as a class. Collect the papers for recording the grades.

Activity #2

Give students about fifteen minutes to preview the study questions for Progress Report 11 and do the related vocabulary work.

Activity #3

Have students read Progress Report 11 for the rest of the period. If you have not completed the oral reading evaluations, do so now. If the evaluations have been completed, you may want the students to read silently. If students do not complete the reading assignment in class, they should do so prior to your next class meeting.

## ORAL READING EVALUATION  *Flowers for Algernon*

Name_____Class_____Date _____

| SKILL | EXCELLENT | GOOD | AVERAGE | FAIR | POOR |
|---|---|---|---|---|---|
| Fluency | 5 | 4 | 3 | 2 | 1 |
| Clarity | 5 | 4 | 3 | 2 | 1 |
| Audibility | 5 | 4 | 3 | 2 | 1 |
| Pronunciation | 5 | 4 | 3 | 2 | 1 |
| _____ | 5 | 4 | 3 | 2 | 1 |
| _____ | 5 | 4 | 3 | 2 | 1 |

Total _____ Grade _____

Comments:

## LESSON FIVE

Objectives
1. To give students the opportunity to practice writing to persuade
2. To give the teacher the opportunity to evaluate each student's writing skills

Activity #1
Distribute Writing Assignment #1 and discuss the directions in detail. Allow the remaining class time for students to work on the assignment. Give students an additional two or three days to complete the assignment, if necessary.

Activity #2
Distribute copies of the Writing Evaluation Form (included in this Unit Plan.) Explain to students that during Lesson Nine you will be holding individual writing conferences about this writing assignment. Make sure they are familiar with the criteria on the Writing Evaluation Form.

Follow-Up: After you have graded the assignments, have a writing conference with each student, (This unit schedules one in Lesson Nine.) After the writing conference, allow students to revise their papers using your suggestions to complete the revision. I suggest grading the revisions on an A-C-E scale (all revisions well-done, some revisions made, few or no revisions made.) This will speed your grading time and still give some credit for the students' efforts.

## LESSON SIX

Objectives
1. To review the main ideas and events in Progress Report 11
2. To preview the study questions and vocabulary for Progress Reports 12-13
3. To read Progress Reports 12-13 silently

Activity #1
Ask students to get out their books and some paper (not their study guides.) Tell them to write down ten questions and answers which cover the main events and ideas in Progress Report 11. Discuss the students' questions and answers orally, making a list on the board of the questions with brief responses. Put a star next to students' questions and answers that are essentially the same as the study guide questions. Be sure that all of the study guide questions are answered.

Activity #2
Give students about fifteen minutes to do the prereading and vocabulary work for Progress Reports 12-13.

Activity #3
Give students the remainder of the period to begin silently reading Progress Reports 12-13. Remind them that the reading must be completed prior to your next class meeting.

# WRITING ASSIGNMENT #1 *Flowers for Algernon*

## PROMPT

At the beginning of the novel, Charlie was being considered for a special scientific experiment. He told the doctors why he wanted to be chosen. Alice Kinnian also recommended him. A research hospital near you has recently tested a method for increasing intelligence in animals. Now they are ready to experiment on a human being. You want to be chosen for the experiment. You must write a letter to the doctor conducting the experiment explaining why you are the best candidate for the procedure.

## PREWRITING

The first thing you need to do is think about why you want to have the procedure done. What is your motivation?

Next, make a list of the reasons you are a good choice for the experiment. Include things like current health, and contributions you have already made to your school or community. How will increasing your intelligence help you? How will you use your new abilities to help others?

When you have finished your list, arrange the items in the order in which you want to present them.

## DRAFTING-

In the first paragraph, introduce yourself and tell what you want. Next, give more background about yourself, including the reasons you think you are a good choice for the experiment. You may want to use one paragraph for each reason. Make sure to include details and examples to explain your reasons. Write a paragraph telling how you will use your new intelligence to help others. In your concluding paragraph, restate your desire to be chosen. Thank the readers for their time.

## PROMPT

When you finish the rough draft of your paper, ask another student to read it. After reading your rough draft, he/she should tell you what he/she liked best about your work, which parts were difficult to understand, and ways in which your work could be improved. Reread your paper considering your critic's comments, and make the corrections you think are necessary.

You may want another student to look at your display. Ask for information about its neatness and attractiveness.

## PROOFREADING

Do a final proofreading of your paper, double-checking your grammar, spelling, organization, and the clarity of your ideas.

# WRITING EVALUATION FORM *Flowers for Algernon*

Name _____ Date _____ Class _____

Writing Assignment #1 for *Flowers for Algernon*

Circle One For Each Item:

| | | | | |
|---|---|---|---|---|
| Introduction | excellent | good | fair | poor |
| Body Paragraphs | excellent | good | fair | poor |
| Summary | excellent | good | fair | poor |
| Grammar | excellent | good | fair | poor (errors noted) |
| Spelling | excellent | good | fair | poor (errors noted) |
| Punctuation | excellent | good | fair | poor (errors noted) |
| Legibility | excellent | good | fair | poor (errors noted) |

Strengths:


Weaknesses:


Comments/Suggestions:

## LESSON SEVEN

Objectives
    1. To review the study guide questions and answers for Progress Reports 12-13
    2. To preview the study questions and vocabulary for Progress Report 14
    3. To read Progress Report 14

Activity #1
    Review the study guide questions and answers for Progress Reports 12-13.

Activity #2
    Give students about fifteen minutes to complete the prereading and vocabulary work for Progress Report 14.

Activity #3
    Depending on the needs of your group, have the students read these chapters orally or silently. Remind them that any reading not completed in class must be finished before the next class meeting.

## LESSON EIGHT

Objectives
    1. To review the main ideas and events from Progress Report 14
    2. To introduce Writing Assignment #2

Activity #1
    Go over the study guide questions and answers for Progress Report 14.

Activity #2
    Distribute Writing Assignment #2. Discuss the directions in detail and give students ample time to complete the assignment.

## LESSON NINE

<u>Objectives</u>
    1. To have students revise their first writing assignment papers
    2. To work on other assignments independently

<u>Activity #1</u>
    Call students to your desk or some other private area to discuss their papers from Writing Assignment #1. Use the completed Writing Evaluation Form as a basis for your critique.

<u>Activity #2</u>
    Students should use this period (when they are not conferencing with you) to work on their Nonfiction assignment, or to review the study guide questions they have covered so far.

# WRITING ASSIGNMENT #2 *Flowers for Algernon*

## PROMPT

You are an energetic young newspaper reporter looking for the big story that will launch your career. You often stop in the Mr. Donner's bakery on your way to the office. One morning, you notice that Charlie seems different than before. He is more talkative. He almost seems more intelligent. You begin a conversation with him, and he starts telling you his story. This could be your big break! You eagerly begin taking notes.

## PREWRITING

Before you write, read several news articles to become familiar with the format. Then, think of questions you want to ask Charlie. Remember to use the newspaper writer's 5W and H questions: who, what, when, where, why, and how. Reread the novel to find the answers to your questions. Take accurate notes. Newspaper reporters must have their facts straight. You can also interpret information in the novel to talk about Charlie's feelings.

## DRAFTING

Think of a catchy headline. It should include the main idea of the article, and make people want to read it. In the first paragraph, present the most important facts-what happened, and to whom it happened. Follow this with paragraphs that explain the procedure and the outcome. You may also want to include quotes from Charlie, Alice and the doctors, giving their opinions about the procedure.

Make your paper look authentic. Use a real newspaper article as a model. You may want to use a computer program to design your layout.

## PROMPT

When you finish the rough draft of your paper, ask another student to read it. After reading your rough draft, he/she should tell you what he/she liked best about your work, which parts were difficult to understand, and ways in which your work could be improved. Reread your paper considering your critic's comments, and make the corrections you think are necessary.

## PROOFREADING

Do a final proofreading of your paper double-checking your grammar, spelling, organization, and the clarity of your ideas.

## LESSON TEN

### Objectives
1. To complete the prereading and vocabulary work for Progress Reports 15-16
2. To silently read Progress Reports 15-16

### Activity #1
Give students about fifteen minutes to preview the study questions and do the related vocabulary work.

### Activity #2
Have students read the chapters silently and answer the study guide questions.

## LESSON ELEVEN

### Objectives
1. To preview the study questions and vocabulary for Progress Report 17
2. To read Progress Report 17

### Activity #1
Give students about fifteen minutes to complete the prereading and vocabulary work for Progress Report 17.

### Activity #2
Depending on the needs of your group, have the students read these chapters orally or silently. Remind them that any reading not completed in class must be finished before the next class meeting.

## LESSON TWELVE

Objective
> To discuss *Flowers for Algernon* at the interpretive and critical levels

Activity #1
> Choose the questions from the Extra Writing Assignments/Discussion Questions which seem most appropriate for your students. A class discussion of these questions is most effective if students have been given the opportunity to formulate answers to the questions prior to the discussion. To this end, you may either have all the students formulate answers to all the questions, divide the class into groups and assign one or more questions to each group, or you could assign one questions to each student in your class. The option you choose will make a difference in the amount of class time needed for this activity.

Activity #2
> After students have had ample time to formulate answers to the questions, begin your class discussion of the questions and the ideas presented by the questions. Be sure students take notes during the discussion so they have information to study for the unit test.

## LESSON THIRTEEN

Objectives
> 1. To introduce Writing Assignment #3
> 2. To give students time to work on the writing assignment

Activity #1
> Distribute copies of Writing Assignment #3. Discuss the directions in detail and give students ample time to complete the assignment.

## LESSON FOURTEEN

Objectives
> 1. To give students the opportunity to do research for their Nonfiction Assignment
> 2. To assist students in the proper use of the school library

Activity
> Take your class to the library for the entire class period. Tell them they can have the time to work on their Nonfiction Assignment. Students who have completed the assignment can use the time to read for pleasure.

# EXTRA WRITING ASSIGNMENT/ DISCUSSION QUESTIONS
*Flowers for Algernon*

Interpretive
1. What are the main conflicts in the story, and how are they resolved?

2. Based on the facts in the story, can you tell approximately in what year the story takes place? Does it matter?

3. Discuss the main themes in the novel.

4. Give a complete character analysis of one of the following: Charlie, Alice, Fay, Professor Nemur, Dr. Strauss.

5. Discuss the use of emotions in the novel.

6. Where is the climax of the novel? Justify your answer.

7. Which events in the novel are "turning points" which affect the course of the plot?

8. Why was Burt upset that Charlie wanted to visit the Warren School?

9. What does the bakery employees' treatment of Charlie after he got smarter say about society?

10. When do you think the novel takes place? Were there any clues in the novel that helped you reach this conclusion?

Critical
11. Explain the significance of the title *Flowers for Algernon*.

12. Do any of the characters change in the course of the novel? If so, who, and how?

13. How did the use of dreams and memories further the plot and character development in the novel?

14. Describe Keyes' writing style. How does it influence our perception of the story?

15. Is the story of *Flowers for Algernon* believable? Why or why not?

16. Is the character of Charlie believable?

17. What comments about the treatment of mentally handicapped people in our society does the novel make?

    Personal Response
18. Did you enjoy the novel? Why or why not?

19. Would you recommend this book to a friend?

20. How did you feel about Charlie as a person?

21. Did you like the way the doctors treated Charlie? Why or why not?

22. Did you like the ending of the novel? Why or why not?

23. What do you think will happen with the research that Charlie completed before he regressed?

24. What do you think will happen to Charlie?

# QUOTATIONS  *Flowers for Algernon*

Discuss the significance of the following quotations.

1. prof Nemur said but why did you want to lern to reed and spell in the frist place. I tolld him because all my life I wantid to be smart and not dumb and my mom always tolld me to try and lern just like Miss Kinnian tells me but its very hard to be smart and even when I lern something in Miss Kinnian's class at the school I ferget lot.

2. And he said that meens Im doing somthing grate for sience and Ill be famus and my name will go down in the books. I don't care so much about beeing famus. I just want to be smart like the other pepul so I can have lots of frends who like me.

3. And she said mabey they got no rite to make me smart because if god wantid me to be smart he would have made me born that way. . . . and mabey Prof Nemur and Dr Strauss was tampiring with things they got no rite to tampir with.

4. Then I was gone to try and find my mom and dad. They woud be serprised to see how smart I got because my mom always wanted me too be smart to. mabey they wouldnt send me away no more if they see how smart I am.

5. Some times somebody will say hey lookit Frank, or Joe or even Gimpy. He really pulled a Charlie Gordon that time. I don't know why they say it but they always laff and I laff too.

6. She said for a person who God gave so little to you did more than a lot of people with brains they never even used.

7. So even if I'm getting intelligent and learning a lot of new things, he thinks I'm still a boy about women. It's confusing, but I'm going to find out all about my life.

8. And then Nemur: "We've predicted the pattern correctly so far. We're justified in making an interim report. I tell you, Jay, there's nothing to be afraid of. We've succeeded. It's all positive. Nothing can go wrong now."

9. Now I understand one of the important reasons for going to college and getting an education is to learn that the things you've believed in all your life aren't true, and that nothing is what it appears to be.

10. "You're fooling yourself, Rose. It's not fair to us or to him. Pretending he's normal. Driving him as if he were an animal that could learn to do tricks. Why don't you leave him alone?"

## QUOTATIONS  *Flowers for Algernon*

11. "Be patient. Don't forget you're accomplishing in weeks what takes others a lifetime. You're a giant sponge soaking in knowledge. Soon you'll begin to connect things up, and you'll see how all the different worlds of learning are related."

12. "Charlie, you amaze me. In some ways you're so advanced, and yet when it comes to making a decision, you're still a child. I can't decide for you, Charlie. The answer can't be found in books-or be solved by bringing it to other people."

13. "I'll tell you what you did, *Mister* Gordon. You come pushing in here with your ideas and suggestions and make the rest of us all look like a bunch of dopes. But I'll tell you something. To me you're still a moron. Maybe I don't understand some of them big words or the names of the books, but I'm as good as you are-better even."

14. "That's not true. But I realize there's nothing we can do. When you've got a child like him it's a cross, and you bear it, and love it. Well, I can bear him, but I can't stand your foolish ways."

15. "But he's put his whole life into this. He's no Freud or Jung or Pavlov or Watson, but he's doing something important and I respect his dedication-maybe even more because he's just an ordinary man trying to do a great man's work, while the great men are all busy making bombs."

16. "Do you think this is easy? Why are you making it harder for me? All these years everyone telling me he should be put away. Well, they were right. Put him away. Maybe at the Home with his own kind he'll have something. I don't know what's right or wrong any more. All I know is I'm not going to sacrifice my daughter for him now."

17. "Not what I expected. No sex, or anything like that. But you were phenomenal. What an act! The weirdest. You'd be great on the stage. You'd wow them at the Palace. You went all confused and silly."

18. "This work is important now, Charlie. Not only to the world and millions of unknown people, but to you. Charlie, you've got to solve this thing for yourself as well. Don't let anyone tie your hands.'

19. "You're feeling sorry for yourself. What did you expect? This experiment was calculated to raise your intelligence, not to make you popular. We had no control over what happened to your personality, and you've developed from a likable, retarded young man into an arrogant, self-centered, antisocial bastard."

20. "Oh, Charlie I'm glad you're back now. We've needed someone. I'm so tired. . . . "

21. "I'm not here because I feel sorry for you. It's because I feel sorry for me."

22. ". . . Charlie if anyone bothers you or trys to take advantage of you call me or Joe or Frank and we will set them strait. We all want you to remember that you got frends here and dont you ever forget it."

23. Anyway I bet im the frist dumb persen in the world who found out some thing inportent for sience. I did somthing but I dont remembir what. So I gess its like I did it for all the dumb pepul like me in Warren and all over the world.

# WRITING ASSIGNMENT # 3 *Flowers for Algernon*

## PROMPT

While Charlie was in the hospital recovering from the surgery, the nurse gave her opinion of the experiment: "Maybe they got no rite to make me smart because if god wantid me to be smart he would have made me born that way. And what about Adem and Eev and the sin with the tree of knowlege and eating the appel and the fall. And mabey Prof Nemur and Dr Strauss was tampiring with the things they got no rite to tampir with."
what is your opinion? Should doctors and scientists tamper with intelligence?

## PREWRITING

The first thing you should do is take a position: yes, doctors and scientists should tamper with intelligence; or no, doctors and scientists should not tamper with intelligence. Jot down the main points you want to make. List facts to support your case. You may want to do some reading, and list quotes and summaries of the opinions of others who agree with your opinion. Decide which points are your strongest and which are weaker. Organize your points from weakest to strongest.

## DRAFTING

Organize your ideas into a rough outline. In the first paragraph, give a little bit of background about he experiment in the story. Then state your opinion. Follow that with one paragraph for each of the main points you have to support your case. Fill in the paragraphs with examples and facts which support your main point. Then, write a paragraph in which you restate your opinion and make your closing statement.

## PROMPT

After you have finished a rough draft of your letter, revise it until you are happy with your work. Then ask another student to tell you what he/she likes best about your work, and what things he/she thinks can be improved. Take another look at your letter, keeping in mind your critic's suggestions, and make the revisions you feel are necessary.

## PROOFREADING

Do a final proofreading of your paper double-checking your grammar, spelling, organization, and the clarity of your ideas.

## LESSON FIFTEEN

### Objective
To review all of the vocabulary work done in this unit

### VOCABULARY REVIEW ACTIVITIES

1. Divide your class into two teams and have an old-fashioned spelling or definition bee.

2. Give each of your students (or students in groups of two, three or four) a *Flowers for Algernon* Vocabulary Word Search Puzzle. The person (group) to find all of the vocabulary words in the puzzle first wins.

3. Give students a *Flowers for Algernon* Vocabulary Word Search Puzzle without the word list. The person or group to find the most vocabulary words in the puzzle wins.

4. Use a *Flowers for Algernon* Vocabulary Crossword Puzzle. Put the puzzle onto a transparency on the overhead projector (so everyone can see it), and do the puzzle together as a class.

5. Give students a *Flowers for Algernon* Vocabulary Matching Worksheet to do.

6. Divide your class into two teams. Use the *Flowers for Algernon* vocabulary words with their letters jumbled as a word list. Student 1 from Team A faces off against Student 1 from Team B. You write the first jumbled word on the board. The first student (1A or 1B) to unscramble the word wins the chance for his/her team to score points. If 1A wins the jumble, go to student 2A and give him/her a definition. He/she must give you the correct spelling of the vocabulary word which fits that definition. If he/she does, Team A scores a point, and you give student 3A a definition for which you expect a correctly spelled matching vocabulary word. Continue giving Team A definitions until some team member makes an incorrect response. An incorrect response sends the game back to the jumbled-word face off, this time with students 2A and 2B. Instead of repeating giving definitions to the first few students of each team, continue with the student after the one who gave the last incorrect response on the team. For example, if Team B wins the jumbled-word face-off, and student 5B gave the last incorrect answer for Team B, you would start this round of definition questions with student 6B, and so on. The team with the most points wins!

7. Have students write a story in which they correctly use as many vocabulary words as possible. Have students read their compositions orally. Post the most original compositions on your bulletin board!

## LESSON SIXTEEN

Objectives
    1. To watch the movie version of Flowers for Algernon
    2. To compare and contrast the movie and the book

Activity #1

    Watch "Charly," which is the movie version of Flowers for Algernon. It is available on video.

Activity #2

    Compare and contrast the movie and the book. Discuss the changes, and the possible reasons for them.

## LESSON SEVENTEEN

Objectives
    1. To widen the breadth of students' knowledge about the topics discussed or touched upon in *Flowers for Algernon*
    2. To check students' non-fiction assignments

Activity

    Ask each student to give a brief oral report about the nonfiction work he/she read for the nonfiction assignment. Your criteria for evaluating this report will vary depending on the level of your students. You may wish for students to give a complete report without using notes of any kind, or you may want students to read directly from a written report, or you may want to do something in between these two extremes. Just make students aware of your criteria in ample time for them to prepare their reports.

    Start with one student's report. After that, ask if anyone else in the class has read on a topic related to the first student's report. If no one has, choose another student at random. After each report, be sure to ask if anyone has a report related to the one just completed. That will help keep a continuity during the discussion of the reports.

## LESSON EIGHTEEN

Objective
    To review the main ideas presented in *Flowers for Algernon*

Activity #1

    Choose one of the review games/activities included in the packet and spend your class period as outlined there.

Activity #2

    Remind students of the date for the Unit Test. Stress the review of the Study Guides and their class notes as a last minute, brush-up review for homework.

# REVIEW GAMES/ACTIVITIES

1. Ask the class to make up a unit test for *Flowers for Algernon*. The test should have 4 sections: multiple choice, true/false, short answer and essay. Students may use 1/2 period to make the test, including a separate answer sheet, and then swap papers and use the other 1/2 class period to take a test a classmate has devised (open book).

2. Take 1/2 period for students to make up true and false questions (including the answers.) Collect the papers and divide the class into two teams. Draw a big tic-tac-toe board on the chalk board. Make one team X and one team O. Ask questions to each side, giving each student one turn. If the question is answered correctly, that student's team's letter (X or O) is placed in the box. If the answer is incorrect, no mark is placed in the box. The object is to get three marks in a row like tic-tac-toe. You may want to keep track of the number of games won for each team.

3. Take 1/2 period for students to make up questions (true/false and short answer). Collect the questions. Divide the class into two teams. You'll alternate asking questions to individual members of teams A & B (like in a spelling bee.) The question keeps going from A to B until it is correctly answered, then a new question is asked. A correct answer does not allow the team to get another question. Correct answers are +2 points; incorrect answers are -1 point.

4. Allow students time to quiz each other (in pairs) from their study guides and class notes.

5. Give students a *Flowers for Algernon* crossword puzzle to complete.

6. Divide your class into two teams. Use the *Flowers for Algernon* crossword words with their letters jumbled as a word list. Student 1 from Team A faces off against Student 1 from Team B. You write the first jumbled word on the board. The first student (1A or 1B) to unscramble the word wins the chance for his/her team to score points. If 1A wins the jumble, go to student 2A and give him/her a clue. He/she must give you the correct word which matches that clue. If he/she does, Team A scores a point, and you give student 3A a clue for which you expect another correct response. Continue giving Team A clues until some team member makes an incorrect response. An incorrect response sends the game back to the jumbled-word face off, this time with students 2A and 2B. Instead of repeating giving clues to the first few students of each team, continue with the student after the one who gave the last incorrect response on the team.

7. Take on the persona of "The Answer Person." Allow students to ask any question about the book. Answer the questions, or tell students where to look in the book to find the answer.

## REVIEW GAMES/ACTIVITIES

8. Students may enjoy playing charades with events from the story. Select a student to start. Give him/her a card with a scene or event from the story. Allow the players to use their books to find the scene being described. The first person to guess each charade performs the next one.

9. Play a categories-type quiz game. (A master is included in this Unit Plan.) Make an overhead transparency of the categories form. Divide the class into teams of three or four players each. Have each team choose a recorder and a score-keeper. Choose a team to go first. That team will choose a category and point amount. Ask the question to the entire class. (Use the Study Guide Quiz and Vocabulary questions.) Give the teams one minute to discuss the answer and write it down. Walk around the room and check the answers. Each team that answers correctly receives the points. (Incorrect answers are not penalized; they just don't receive any points.) Cross out that square on the playing board. Play continues until all squares have been used. The winning team is the one with the most points. You can assign bonus points to any square or squares you choose.

10. Have students complete the last column (What I Learned) of the KWL sheet you distributed in Lesson One. Discuss their answers with the class.

11. Play a picture identification game. Have students draw one scene each from the story. Then have them show their drawings, one at a time, to the rest of the class. The viewers should look through their books to find the scene that is shown in the drawing, then read pertinent passages aloud to the class, or summarize the events surrounding the drawing.

NOTE: If students do not need the extra review, omit this lesson and go on to the test.

QUIZ GAME
*Flowers for Algernon*

| 1-8 | 9-10 | 11-13 | 14 | 15-16 | 17 |
|---|---|---|---|---|---|
| 100 | 100 | 100 | 100 | 100 | 100 |
| 200 | 200 | 200 | 200 | 200 | 200 |
| 300 | 300 | 300 | 300 | 300 | 300 |
| 400 | 400 | 400 | 400 | 400 | 400 |
| 500 | 500 | 500 | 500 | 500 | 500 |

# LESSON NINETEEN

Objective
    To test the students' understanding of the main ideas and themes in *Flowers for Algernon*

Activity #1
    Distribute the *Flowers for Algernon* Unit Tests. Go over the instructions in detail and allow the students the entire class period to complete the exam.

Activity #2
    Collect all test papers and assigned books prior to the end of the class period.


## NOTES ABOUT THE UNIT TESTS IN THIS UNIT:
There are 5 different unit tests which follow.

There are two short answer tests which are based primarily on facts from the novel. The answer key for short answer unit test 1 follows the student test. The answer key for short answer test 2 follows the student short answer unit test 2.

There is one advanced short answer unit test. It is based on the extra discussion questions. Use the matching key for short answer unit test 2 to check the matching section of the advanced short answer unit test. There is no key for the short answer questions. The answers will be based on the discussions you have had during class.

There are two multiple choice unit tests. Following the two unit tests, you will find an answer sheet on which students should mark their answers. The same answer sheet should be used for both tests; however, students' answers will be different for each test. Following the students' answer sheet for the multiple choice tests you will find your answer keys.

The short answer tests have a vocabulary section. You should choose 20 of the vocabulary words from this unit, read them orally and have the students write them down. Then, either have students write a definition or use the words in sentences.

# UNIT TESTS

# SHORT ANSWER UNIT TEST 1 *Flowers for Algernon*

## 1. Matching/ Identify

____ 1.  Charlie Gordon         A.  administered inkblot and other tests
____ 2.  Alice Kinnian          B.  full of life and excitement
____ 3.  Professor Nemur        C.  Charlie's guardian and employer
____ 4.  Burt Selden            D.  wanted to be smart to have people like him
____ 5.  Algernon               E.  rejected her son when a normal daughter was born
____ 6.  Fay Lillman            F.  psychiatrist and neurosurgeon
____ 7.  Dr. Strauss            G.  mouse with increased intelligence
____ 8.  Mr. Donner             H.  "an ordinary man trying to do a great man's work"
____ 9.  Norma Gordon           I.  Charlie's normal sister
____ 10. Rose Gordon            J.  teacher with whom Charlie fell in love

## II. Short Answer

1. What did Alice Kinnian tell the doctors about Charlie?




2. What did Charlie discover at the party he went to with Joe and Frank?

### Short Answer Unit Test 1 *Flowers for Algernon*

3. What did Charlie realize from his nightmare about the bloody knife and the free association he did afterward?

4. What was Charlie's main resentment concerning Professor Nemur?

5. Describe Charlie's visit to Matt Gordon's barbershop.

6. Describe Charlie's relationship with Fay Lillman.

Short Answer Unit Test 1 *Flowers for Algernon*

7. Charlie visited Alice after he had returned from the conference, and established himself in his new apartment. What insight did he share with her during their meeting?

8. Mrs. Nemur held a cocktail party and invited Charlie. During the party, Dr. Strauss described a situation that had come up in Charlie's recent therapy sessions. What was it?

9. Describe Charlie's visit with his mother and his sister.

10. What was the end result of the surgery the doctors performed on Charlie?

## Short Answer Unit Test 1 *Flowers for Algernon*

### III. Essay

How did the use of dreams and memories further the plot and character development in the novel?

## Short Answer Unit Test 1 *Flowers for Algernon*

### IV. Vocabulary

Listen to the vocabulary words and spell them. After you have spelled all the words, go back and write down the definitions.

| WORD | DEFINITION |
|---|---|
| 1. | |
| 2. | |
| 3. | |
| 4. | |
| 5. | |
| 6. | |
| 7. | |
| 8. | |
| 9. | |
| 10. | |
| 11. | |
| 12. | |
| 13. | |
| 14. | |
| 15. | |
| 16. | |
| 17. | |
| 18. | |
| 19. | |
| 20. | |

# ANSWER KEY SHORT ANSWER UNIT TEST 1 *Flowers for Algernon*

| | | | | |
|---|---|---|---|---|
| D | 1. | Charlie Gordon | A. | administered inkblot and other tests |
| J | 2. | Alice Kinnian | B. | full of life and excitement |
| H | 3. | Professor Nemur | C. | Charlie's guardian and employer |
| A | 4. | Burt Selden | D. | wanted to be smart to have people like him |
| G | 5. | Algernon | E. | rejected her son when a normal daughter was born |
| B | 6. | Fay Lillman | F. | psychiatrist and neurosurgeon |
| F | 7. | Dr. Strauss | G. | mouse with increased intelligence |
| C | 8. | Mr. Donner | H. | "an ordinary man trying to do a great man's work" |
| I | 9. | Norma Gordon | I. | Charlie's normal sister |
| E | 10. | Rose Gordon | J. | teacher with whom Charlie fell in love |

1. What did Alice Kinnian tell the doctors about Charlie?
    She said Charlie was her best student. He wanted to learn to read and write even more than some people who were smarter than he was.

2. What did Charlie discover at the party he went to with Joe and Frank?
    He realized they were making fun of him.

3. What did Charlie realize from his nightmare about the bloody knife and the free association he did afterward?
    He realized that he was not ready to think of a woman romantically or sexually. He also realized that he was a person before the surgery, and he wanted to love someone.

4. What was Charlie's main resentment concerning Professor Nemur?
    Charlie resented Nemur's constant references to having made Charlie what he was, of referring to him as less than a human being. Nemur did not recognize that Charlie was a human being even before the surgery.

5. Describe Charlie's visit to Matt Gordon's barbershop.
    He had Matt give him a shave and a haircut. Then Charlie asked Matt if he recognized him. Matt thought Charlie was playing a trick. Charlie tried to tell Matt who he was, but he got lightheaded and felt sick. He left without telling Matt who he was.

6. Describe Charlie's relationship with Fay Lillman.
    She was his neighbor across the hall. He thought she was fun and full of life. They eventually had a sexual relationship, although he did not love her. They drank and went dancing. He did not tell her about himself, because he did not think she would understand.

7. Charlie visited Alice after he had returned from the conference, and established himself in his new apartment. What insight did he share with her during their meeting?

He told her it was not his intelligence that was coming between them, but his emotional state. He was still reacting to her as the child Charlie who was afraid of women because of the things his mother had done to him.

8. Mrs. Nemur held a cocktail party and invited Charlie. During the party, Dr. Strauss described a situation that had come up in Charlie's recent therapy sessions. What was it?

He told the others about Charlie's experiences perceiving himself as he was before the experiment, a separate and distinct individual in the adult Charlie's consciousness.

9. Describe Charlie's visit with his mother and his sister.

Rose was not in total command of her mental faculties. She eventually recognized him, but kept forgetting that she did. She would start raving at the child Charlie, then come back to reality and talk to the adult Charlie.

Norma recognized Charlie and was glad to see him. She told him that their mother had told her he had died in the Warren School. Norma wanted Charlie to take care of her and her mother.

10. What was the end result of the surgery the doctors performed on Charlie?

His intelligence increased for several months, then it started decreasing. At the end of the novel, Charlie was back at about the same intellectual level where he was at the beginning.

# SHORT ANSWER UNIT TEST 2 *Flowers for Algernon*

## 1. Matching/ Identify

| | | | |
|---|---|---|---|
| _____ 1. | Burt Selden | A. | psychiatrist and neurosurgeon |
| _____ 2. | Dr. Strauss | B. | full of life and excitement |
| _____ 3. | Charlie Gordon | C. | Charlie's guardian and employer |
| _____ 4. | Norma Gordon | D. | Charlie's normal sister |
| _____ 5. | Fay Lillman | E. | mouse with increased intelligence |
| _____ 6. | Professor Nemur | F. | administered inkblot and other tests |
| _____ 7. | Algernon | G. | wanted to be smart to have people like him |
| _____ 8. | Mr. Donner | H. | teacher with whom Charlie fell in love |
| _____ 9. | Alice Kinnian | I. | rejected her son when a normal daughter was born |
| _____ 10. | Rose Gordon | J. | "an ordinary man trying to do a great man's work" |

## II. Short Answer

1. What type of surgery did the doctors perform on Charlie, and what was the end result?




2. What was Charlie's request in his last progress report?

Short Answer Unit Test 2 *Flowers for Algernon*

3. Describe Charlie's visit with his mother and his sister.

4. What happened at Mrs. Nemur's cocktail party?

5. Describe Charlie's relationship with Fay Lillman.

6. What changes happened at the bakery when Charlie started getting smarter?

Short Answer Unit Test 2 *Flowers for Algernon*

7. Charlie visited Alice after he had returned from the conference, and established himself in his new apartment. What insight did he share with her during their meeting?

8. What did Charlie find confusing about his dreams and memories?

9. What did Alice Kinnian tell the doctors about Charlie?

10. What did Charlie discover in his conversations with various professors and specialists?

Short Answer Unit Test 2 *Flowers for Algernon*

III. Essay

    What are the main conflicts in the novel, and how are they resolved?

Short Answer Unit Test 2 *Flowers for Algernon*

## IV. Vocabulary

Listen to the vocabulary words and spell them. After you have spelled all the words, go back and write down the definitions.

| **WORD** | **DEFINITION** |
|---|---|
| 1._____ | _____ |
| 2._____ | _____ |
| 3._____ | _____ |
| 4._____ | _____ |
| 5._____ | _____ |
| 6._____ | _____ |
| 7._____ | _____ |
| 8._____ | _____ |
| 9._____ | _____ |
| 10._____ | _____ |
| 11._____ | _____ |
| 12._____ | _____ |
| 13._____ | _____ |
| 14._____ | _____ |
| 15._____ | _____ |
| 16._____ | _____ |
| 17._____ | _____ |
| 18._____ | _____ |
| 19._____ | _____ |
| 20._____ | _____ |

# ANSWER KEY SHORT ANSWER UNIT TEST 2 *Flowers for Algernon*
Also use the answer key for this matching test for the advanced short answer matching test

## I. Matching/Identify

| | | | | |
|---|---|---|---|---|
| F | 1. | Burt Selden | A. | psychiatrist and neurosurgeon |
| A | 2. | Dr. Strauss | B. | full of life and excitement |
| G | 3. | Charlie Gordon | C. | Charlie's guardian and employer |
| D | 4. | Norma Gordon | D. | Charlie's normal sister |
| B | 5. | Fay Lillman | E. | mouse with increased intelligence |
| J | 6. | Professor Nemur | F. | administered inkblot and other tests |
| E | 7. | Algernon | G. | wanted to be smart to have people like him |
| C | 8. | Mr. Donner | H. | teacher with whom Charlie fell in love |
| H | 9. | Alice Kinnian | I. | rejected her son when a normal daughter was born |
| I | 10. | Rose Gordon | J. | "an ordinary man trying to do a great man's work" |

## II. Short Answer

1. What type of surgery did the doctors perform on Charlie, and what was the end result?
    It was an experimental surgery designed to increase intelligence. It had been performed on a mouse but never before on a human. Charlie's intelligence increased for several months, then it started decreasing. At the end of the novel, Charlie was back at about the same intellectual level where he was at the beginning.

2. What was Charlie's request in his last progress report?
    He asked that someone put flowers on Algernon's grave.

3. Describe Charlie's visit with his mother and his sister.
    Rose was not in total command of her mental faculties. She eventually recognized him, but kept forgetting that she did. She would start raving at the child Charlie, then come back to reality and talk to the adult Charlie.
    Norma recognized Charlie and was glad to see him. She told him that their mother had told her he had died in the Warren School. Norma wanted Charlie to take care of her and her mother.

4. What happened at Mrs. Nemur's cocktail party?
    Charlie got drunk, and was rude to the other guests. Nemur, Strauss, and Burt became very angry with him. They accused him of endangering their work. Charlie accused them of not caring about him as a person.

5. Describe Charlie's relationship with Fay Lillman.
   She was his neighbor across the hall. He thought she was fun and full of life. They eventually had a sexual relationship, although he did not love her. They drank and went dancing. He did not tell her about himself, because he did not think she would understand.

6. What changes happened at the bakery when Charlie started getting smarter?
   The other men were surprised when Charlie learned to operate the dough machine. When he found a way to speed up production, Mr. Donner gave him a raise and a bonus. The other workers started acting hostile toward Charlie. They didn't like his new intelligence, because they thought he was showing them up.

7. Charlie visited Alice after he had returned from the conference, and established himself in his new apartment. What insight did he share with her during their meeting?
   He told her it was not his intelligence that was coming between them, but his emotional state. He was still reacting to her as the child Charlie who was afraid of women because of the things his mother had done to him.

8. What did Charlie find confusing about his dreams and memories?
   He wasn't sure whether they really happened the way he now remembered, or whether he was remembering the way things seemed at the time. He thought he might be inventing the dreams and memories.

9. What did Alice Kinnian tell the doctors about Charlie?
   She said Charlie was her best student. He wanted to learn to read and write even more than some people who were smarter than he was.

10. What did Charlie discover in his conversations with various professors and specialists?
    He discovered that they didn't know much outside of their own specializations. He was not able to converse with them at the level he had hoped for. He observed that they were not intellectual giants after all, but were only people who were afraid the rest of the world would find out their limitations.

# ADVANCED SHORT ANSWER TEST *Flowers for Algernon*

## 1. Matching/ Identify

_____ 1. Burt Selden  A. psychiatrist and neurosurgeon
_____ 2. Dr. Strauss  B. full of life and excitement
_____ 3. Charlie Gordon  C. Charlie's guardian and employer
_____ 4. Norma Gordon  D. Charlie's normal sister
_____ 5. Fay Lillman  E. mouse with increased intelligence
_____ 6. Professor Nemur  F. administered inkblot and other tests
_____ 7. Algernon  G. wanted to be smart to have people like him
_____ 8. Mr. Donner  H. teacher with whom Charlie fell in love
_____ 9. Alice Kinnian  I. rejected her son when a normal daughter was born
_____ 10. Rose Gordon  J. "an ordinary man trying to do a great man's work"

## II. Short Answer

1. Discuss the main themes in the novel.

2. What comments about the treatment of mentally handicapped people in our society does the novel make?

Advanced Short Answer Test *Flowers for Algernon*

3. How did the use of dreams and memories further the plot and character development in the novel?

4. Give a complete character analysis of one of the following: Charlie, Alice, Fay, Professor Nemur, Dr. Strauss.

5. Explain the significance of the title *Flowers for Algernon*.

### Advanced Short Answer Test *Flowers for Algernon*

### III. Quotations
Explain the importance of the following quotations.

1. Sometimes somebody will say hey lookit Frank, or Joe, or even Gimpy. He really pulled a Charlie Gordon that time. I don't know why they say it but they always laff and I laff also.

2. "You're fooling yourself, Rose. It's not fair to us or to him. Pretending he's normal. Driving him as if he were an animal that could learn to do tricks. Why don't you leave him alone?"

3. "I'll tell you what you did, *Mister* Gordon. You come pushing in here with your ideas and suggestions and make the rest of us all look like a bunch of dopes. But I'll tell you something. To me you're still a moron. Maybe I don't understand some of them big words or the names of the books, but I'm as good as you are-better even."

## Advanced Short Answer Test *Flowers for Algernon*

4. "But he's put his whole life into this. He's no Freud or Jung or Pavlov or Watson, but he's doing something important and I respect his dedication-maybe even more because he's just an ordinary man trying to do a great man's work, while the great men are all busy making bombs."

5. Anyway I bet im the frist dumb persen in the world who found out some thing inportent for sience. I did somthing but I dont remembir what. So I gess its like I did it for all the dumb pepul like me in Warren and all over the world.

## Advanced Short Answer Test *Flowers for Algernon*

IV. Vocabulary

Listen to the vocabulary words and write them down. After you have written down all of the words, write a paragraph in which you use all the words. The paragraph must relate in some way to *Flowers for Algernon*.

# MULTIPLE CHOICE UNIT TEST 1 *Flowers for Algernon*

## 1. Matching/ Identify

____ 1.  Charlie Gordon         A.  administered inkblot and other tests
____ 2.  Alice Kinnian          B.  full of life and excitement
____ 3.  Professor Nemur        C.  Charlie's guardian and employer
____ 4.  Burt Selden            D.  wanted to be smart to have people like him
____ 5.  Algernon               E.  rejected her son when a normal daughter was born
____ 6.  Fay Lillman            F.  psychiatrist and neurosurgeon
____ 7.  Dr. Strauss            G.  mouse with increased intelligence
____ 8.  Mr. Donner             H.  "an ordinary man trying to do a great man's work"
____ 9.  Norma Gordon           I.  Charlie's normal sister
____ 10. Rose Gordon            J.  teacher with whom Charlie fell in love

## II. Multiple Choice

1.  Why was Charlie taking the tests?
    A. He was applying for a permit to live alone without a guardian.
    B. He wanted to be admitted to a special training school.
    C. He hoped the doctors would use him in an experiment to make him smarter.
    D. He wanted to graduate from the adult school.

2.  What did Charlie discover at the party he went to with Joe and Frank?
    A. He thought he was falling in love with Ellen.
    B. He discovered he liked to drink beer.
    C. He found out he was a good dancer.
    D. He realized that they were making fun of him.

3.  What did Charlie realize from his nightmare about the bloody knife and the free association he did after the dream?
    A. He realized he was a person before the surgery, and he wanted to love someone.
    B. He realized he must have been attacked by someone with a knife.
    C. He realized he was reliving the surgery.
    D. He realized he had suicidal tendencies.

4. True or False: Doctors Nemur and Strauss were beginning to treat Charlie like an equal, and ask his opinion about their experiments.
   A. True
   B. False

5. Describe Charlie's observations about Fay Lillman.
   A. He thought she was morally corrupt.
   B. He thought she was attractive and full of life and excitement.
   C. He thought she was boring and dull.
   D. He thought she was the perfect woman for him.

6. Did Charlie reveal himself to his father at the barber shop?
   A. Yes
   B. No

7. What insights did Charlie share with Alice when he finally contacted her?
   A. He said he realized his emotional state was coming between them.
   B. He said he realized his intellectual state was coming between them.
   C. He said he did not have time for women; he had to devote himself to work.
   D. He said he really loved Fay.

8. What happened at Mrs. Nemur's cocktail party?
   A. Charlie made a pass at Mrs. Nemur.
   B. Charlie impressed Mr. Raynor and got another grant.
   C. Charlie got drunk, and was rude to the other guests.
   D. Charlie had a panic attack and hid in the bathroom most of the evening.

9. Which of the following describes Charlie's visit to his mother?
   A. Rose was not in total command of her mental faculties. She would start raving at the child Charlie, then come back to reality and talk to the adult Charlie.
   B. Rose told him her son was dead. She refused to let him in. He left without talking to her.
   C. Rose was glad to see him. They talked for a long time. She explained her fears and feelings from when he was small. They parted on good terms.
   D. Rose refused to believe he got smarter. She thought it was an impostor playing a trick on her. Charlie could not convince her to believe otherwise.

10. What was the length of time that elapses from the first to the last progress report?
    A. three years
    B. fifty-six days
    C. eighteen months
    D. seven months

III. Quotations  Identify the speaker.

A. Charlie          C. Rose Gordon      E. Professor Nemur     G. Fay Lillman
B. Alice Kinnian    D. Matt Gordon      F. Burt Selden         H. Frank

1. "We've predicted the pattern correctly so far. We're justified in making an interim report. I tell you, Jay, there's nothing to be afraid of. We've succeeded. It's all positive. Nothing can go wrong now."

2. "You're fooling yourself. It's not fair to us or to him. Pretending he's normal. Driving him as if he were an animal that could learn to do tricks. Why don't you leave him alone?"

3. "Be patient. Don't forget you're accomplishing in weeks what takes others a lifetime. You're a giant sponge soaking in knowledge. Soon you'll begin to connect things up, and you'll see how all the different worlds of learning are related."

4. "But he's put his whole life into this. He's no Freud or Jung or Pavlov or Watson, but he's doing something important and I respect his dedication-maybe even more because he's just an ordinary man trying to do a great man's work, while the great men are all busy making bombs."

5. "Not what I expected. No sex, or anything like that. But you were phenomenal. What an act! The weirdest. You'd be great on the stage. You'd wow them at the Palace. You went all confused and silly."

6. Anyway I bet im the frist dumb persen in the world who found out some thing inportent for sience. I did somthing but I dont remembir what. So I gess its like I did it for all the dumb pepul like me in Warren and all over the world.

7. So even if I'm getting intelligent and learning a lot of new things, he thinks I'm still a boy about women. It's confusing, but I'm going to find out all about my life.

8. "Do you think this is easy? Why are you making it harder for me? All these years everyone telling me he should be put away. Well, they were right. Put him away. Maybe at the Home with his own kind he'll have something. I don't know what's right or wrong any more. All I know is I'm not going to sacrifice my daughter for him now."

9. "I'll tell you what you did, *Mister* Gordon. You come pushing in here with your ideas and suggestions and make the rest of us all look like a bunch of dopes. But I'll tell you something. To me you're still a moron. Maybe I don't understand some of them big words or the names of the books, but I'm as good as you are-better even."

10. "Charlie, you amaze me. I some ways you're so advanced, and yet when it come to making a decision, you're still a child. I can't decide for you, Charlie. The answer can't be found in books-or be solved by bringing it to other people."

## IV. Vocabulary Matching

1. accumulated
2. admonish
3. berserk
4. consistent
5. cynical
6. deterioration
7. erratic
8. exigencies
9. futile
10. implication
11. inevitable
12. juxtaposition
13. lethargy
14. massive
15. paradoxical
16. phenomenal
17. precaution
18. prognosis
19. stupor
20. usurped

A. diminishing in quality
B. placement side by side for comparison or contrast
C. state of mental numbness
D. having no useful result
E. gathered or piled up
F. large or imposing
G. lacking consistency, regularity, or uniformity
H. to reprove gently but earnestly
I. extraordinary; outstanding
J. that which is hinted at or suggested
K. taken over or occupied without right
L. prediction of a disease's course and outcome
M. sluggishness, apathy, inactivity
N. action taken in advance to prevent danger
O. urgent requirements; pressing needs
P. destructively or frenetically violent
Q. impossible to avoid or prevent
R. expressing scorn and bitter mockery
S. seemingly contradictory but possibly true
T. reliable or uniform

# MULTIPLE CHOICE UNIT TEST 2 *Flowers for Algernon*

## 1. Matching/ Identify

_____ 1.  Burt Selden          A.  psychiatrist and neurosurgeon
_____ 2.  Dr. Strauss          B.  full of life and excitement
_____ 3.  Charlie Gordon       C.  Charlie's guardian and employer
_____ 4.  Norma Gordon         D.  Charlie's normal sister
_____ 5.  Fay Lillman          E.  mouse with increased intelligence
_____ 6.  Professor Nemur      F.  administered inkblot and other tests
_____ 7.  Algernon             G.  wanted to be smart to have people like him
_____ 8.  Mr. Donner           H.  teacher with whom Charlie fell in love
_____ 9.  Alice Kinnian        I.  rejected her son when a normal daughter was born
_____ 10. Rose Gordon          J.  "an ordinary man trying to do a great man's work"

## II. Multiple Choice

1. Why was Charlie taking the tests at the beginning of the novel?
   A. He was applying for a permit to live alone without a guardian.
   B. He wanted to be admitted to a special training school.
   C. He hoped the doctors would use him in an experiment to make him smarter.
   D. He wanted to graduate from the adult school.

2. What was Charlie's request in his last progress report?
   A. He asked Professor Nemur to use his (Charlie's) research to find a way to make him smart again.
   B. He asked Alice to visit him and write letters to him.
   C. He asked that someone put flowers on Algernon's grave.
   D. He asked Burt to make sure Norma got the money in his savings account.

3. Which of the following describes Charlie's visit to his mother?
   A. Rose was not in total command of her mental faculties. She would start raving at the child Charlie, then come back to reality and talk to the adult Charlie.
   B. Rose told him her son was dead. She refused to let him in. He left without talking to her.
   C. Rose was glad to see him. They talked for a long time. She explained her fears and feelings from when he was small. They parted on good terms.
   D. Rose refused to believe he got smarter. She thought it was an impostor playing a trick on her. Charlie could not convince her to believe otherwise.

4. True or False: On the first night they spent together, Charlie told Fay he couldn't play with her because his mother would take away his peanuts and put him in a cage.
   A. True
   B. False

5. What happened at Mrs. Nemur's cocktail party?
   A. Charlie made a pass at Mrs. Nemur.
   B. Charlie impressed Mr. Raynor and got another grant.
   C. Charlie got drunk, and was rude to the other guests.
   D. Charlie had a panic attack and hid in the bathroom most of the evening.

6. What happened when Charlie went back to the bakery?
   A. The other men didn't believe he was no longer smart. They sent him away.
   B. He got scared and didn't go in.
   C. Mr. Donner gave him back his job.
   D. He found out Gimpy was running the bakery. Gimpy would not re-hire him.

7. What insights did Charlie share with Alice when he finally contacted her?
   A. He said he realized his emotional state was coming between them.
   B. He said he realized his intellectual state was coming between them.
   C. He said he did not have time for women; he had to devote himself to work.
   D. He said he really loved Fay.

8. What did Charlie find confusing about his dreams and memories?
   A. He didn't remember some of the people in them.
   B. He didn't know whether or not to talk about them.
   C. He wasn't sure whether they really happened the way he now remembered.
   D. They made him upset, and he never used to get upset.

9. Who said Charlie wanted to learn to read and write even more than some people who were smarter than he was?
   A. Miss Kinnian
   B. Professor Nemur
   C. Mr. Donner
   D. Charlie

10. What did Charlie do at the conference?
    A. He supported Nemur's conclusions in front of Nemur's colleagues.
    B. He released Algernon from his cage, and took him back to New York.
    C. He went berserk and started dancing on the conference table.
    D. He refused to talk to anyone about his life before or after the surgery.

III. Quotations   Identify the Speaker

A. Charlie             C. Rose Gordon        E. Professor Nemur      G. Fay Lillman
B. Alice Kinnian       D. Matt Gordon        F. Burt Selden          H. Frank

1. "Be patient. Don't forget you're accomplishing in weeks what takes others a lifetime. You're a giant sponge soaking in knowledge. Soon you'll begin to connect things up, and you'll see how all the different worlds of learning are related."

2. So even if I'm getting intelligent and learning a lot of new things, he thinks I'm still a boy about women. It's confusing, but I'm going to find out all about my life.

3. "Do you think this is easy? Why are you making it harder for me? All these years everyone telling me he should be put away. Well, they were right. Put him away. Maybe at the Home with his own kind he'll have something. I don't know what's right or wrong any more. All I know is I'm not going to sacrifice my daughter for him now."

4. "Not what I expected. No sex, or anything like that. But you were phenomenal. What an act! The weirdest. You'd be great on the stage. You'd wow them at the Palace. You went all confused and silly."

5. "You're fooling yourself. It's not fair to us or to him. Pretending he's normal. Driving him as if he were an animal that could learn to do tricks. Why don't you leave him alone?"

6. "Charlie, you amaze me. I some ways you're so advanced, and yet when it come to making a decision, you're still a child. I can't decide for you, Charlie. The answer can't be found in books-or be solved by bringing it to other people."

7. "We've predicted the pattern correctly so far. We're justified in making an interim report. I tell you, Jay, there's nothing to be afraid of. We've succeeded. It's all positive. Nothing can go wrong now."

8. Anyway I bet im the frist dumb persen in the world who found out some thing inportent for sience. I did somthing but I dont remembir what. So I gess its like I did it for all the dumb pepul like me in Warren and all over the world.

9. "I'll tell you what you did, *Mister* Gordon. You come pushing in here with your ideas and suggestions and make the rest of us all look like a bunch of dopes. But I'll tell you something. To me you're still a moron. Maybe I don't understand some of them big words or the names of the books, but I'm as good as you are-better even."

10. "But he's put his whole life into this. He's no Freud or Jung or Pavlov or Watson, but he's doing something important and I respect his dedication-maybe even more because he's just an ordinary man trying to do a great man's work, while the great men are all busy making bombs."

## IV. Vocabulary

1. administered
2. amnesia
3. complicated
4. conscious
5. cowers
6. despising
7. docile
8. euphemisms
9. imperceptibly
10. ironic
11. marooned
12. numb
13. obligations
14. obstruction
15. pathology
16. plateau
17. recede
18. superimposed
19. vague
20. valid

A. partial or total loss of memory
B. cringes in fear
C. not aware of
D. mild terms that are substituted for offensive ones
E. something that gets in the way
F. placed on or over something else
G. emotionally unresponsive; indifferent
H. yielding to supervision, direction, or management
I. a departure or deviation from a normal condition
J. disliking intensely
K. producing the desired results
L. not easy to understand
M. given out; dispensed
N. contrary to what is expected or intended
O. to move back or away from
P. duties or promises
Q. abandoned or isolated with little hope of rescue
R. waking awareness perceptible at any given instant
S. indistinctly felt or perceived
T. a stable level, period, or state

ANSWER SHEET   Multiple Choice Unit Tests   *Flowers for Algernon*

| I. Matching | III. Quotations | IV. Vocabulary |
|---|---|---|
| 1. _____ | 1. _____ | 1. _____ |
| 2. _____ | 2. _____ | 2. _____ |
| 3. _____ | 3. _____ | 3. _____ |
| 4. _____ | 4. _____ | 4. _____ |
| 5. _____ | 5. _____ | 5. _____ |
| 6. _____ | 6. _____ | 6. _____ |
| 7. _____ | 7. _____ | 7. _____ |
| 8. _____ | 8. _____ | 8. _____ |
| 9. _____ | 9. _____ | 9. _____ |
| 10. _____ | 10. _____ | 10. _____ |
| | | 11. _____ |
| | | 12. _____ |
| | | 13. _____ |
| | | 14. _____ |
| | | 15. _____ |
| | | 16. _____ |
| | | 17. _____ |
| | | 18. _____ |
| | | 19. _____ |
| | | 20. _____ |

II. Multiple Choice

1.  (A) (B) (C) (D)
2.  (A) (B) (C) (D)
3.  (A) (B) (C) (D)
4.  (A) (B) (C) (D)
5.  (A) (B) (C) (D)
6.  (A) (B) (C) (D)
7.  (A) (B) (C) (D)
8.  (A) (B) (C) (D)
9.  (A) (B) (C) (D)
10. (A) (B) (C) (D)

ANSWER SHEET KEY   Multiple Choice Unit Test 1   Flowers for Algernon

| I. Matching | | III. Quotations | | IV. Vocabulary | |
|---|---|---|---|---|---|
| 1. | D | 1. | E | 1. | E |
| 2. | J | 2. | D | 2. | H |
| 3. | H | 3. | B | 3. | P |
| 4. | A | 4. | F | 4. | T |
| 5. | G | 5. | G | 5. | R |
| 6. | B | 6. | A | 6. | A |
| 7. | F | 7. | A | 7. | G |
| 8. | C | 8. | C | 8. | O |
| 9. | I | 9. | H | 9. | D |
| 10. | E | 10. | B | 10. | J |
| | | | | 11. | Q |
| | | | | 12. | B |
| | | | | 13. | M |
| | | | | 14. | F |
| | | | | 15. | S |
| | | | | 16. | I |
| | | | | 17. | N |
| | | | | 18. | L |
| | | | | 19. | C |
| | | | | 20. | K |

II. Multiple Choice
1.  (A) (B) ( ) (D)
2.  (A) (B) (C) ( )
3.  (...) (B) (C) (D)
4.  (A) ( ) (C) (D)
5.  (A) ( ) (C) (D)
6.  (A) ( ) (C) (D)
7.  ( ) (B) (C) (D)
8.  (A) (B) ( ) (D)
9.  ( ) (B) (C) (D)
10. (A) (B) (C) ( )

ANSWER SHEET KEY   Multiple Choice Unit Test  2  Flowers for Algernon

| I. Matching | III. Quotations | IV. Vocabulary |
|---|---|---|
| 1. F | 1. B | 1. M |
| 2. A | 2. A | 2. A |
| 3. G | 3. C | 3. L |
| 4. D | 4. G | 4. R |
| 5. B | 5. D | 5. B |
| 6. J | 6. B | 6. J |
| 7. E | 7. E | 7. H |
| 8. C | 8. A | 8. D |
| 9. H | 9. H | 9. C |
| 10. I | 10. F | 10. N |
|   |   | 11. Q |
|   |   | 12. G |
|   |   | 13. P |
|   |   | 14. E |
|   |   | 15. I |
|   |   | 16. T |
|   |   | 17. O |
|   |   | 18. F |
|   |   | 19. S |
|   |   | 20. K |

II. Multiple Choice
1.  (A) (B) ( ) (D)
2.  (A) (B) ( ) (D)
3.  ( ) (B) (C) (D)
4.  ( ) (B) (C) (D)
5.  (A) (B) ( ) (D)
6.  ( ) (B) (C) (D)
7.  ( ) (B) (C) (D)
8.  (A) (B) ( ) (D)
9.  ( ) (B) (C) (D)
10. (A) ( ) (C) (D)

# UNIT RESOURCES

## BULLETIN BOARD IDEAS

1. Save one corner of the board for the best of students' *Flowers for Algernon* writing assignments. You may want to use background maps of New York City to represent the setting of the novel.

2. Take one of the word search puzzles from the extra activities packet and with a marker copy it over in a large size on the bulletin board. Write the clue words to find to one side. Invite students prior to and after class to find the words and circle them on the bulletin board.

3. Have students find or draw pictures that they think resemble the people in the book.

4. Invite students to help make an interactive bulletin board quiz. Give each student a half-sheet of paper (about 4"x5') folded in half so that it can open. On the outside flap, have each student write a description of one of the characters in the text. On the inside, they will write the name of the character. You can staple or tack these papers to the bulletin board so that the students can read the descriptions and lift the flaps to find the answers.

5. Make inkblot prints and display them. Have students give their interpretations of what they see in the inkblots.

6. Make a display of pictures of book jackets and artwork from the various editions of *Flowers for Algernon*. You may want to include pictures from the movie version, *Charly*.

7. Cut out or draw pictures of white mice.

8. Display articles about Daniel Keyes and critiques of his work.

9. Have students design postcards depicting the settings of the book.

10. Have students construct a large maze and put it on the bulletin board. Students can use yarn to wind their way through it.

# EXTRA ACTIVITIES  *Flowers for Algernon*

One of the difficulties in teaching a novel is that all students don't read at the same speed. One student who likes to read may take the book home and finish it in a day or two. Sometimes a few students finish the in-class assignments early. The problem, then, is finding suitable extra activities for students.

One thing that helps is to keep a little library in the classroom. For this unit on *Flowers for Algernon*, you might check out from the school or public library other books by Daniel Keyes. There are also many other science fiction novels that students would enjoy reading. Students may also enjoy reading journal articles debating the use of animals for laboratory tests. Magazines such as *Psychology Today*, *Omni*, and *Scientific American* often have articles dealing with the topics mentioned in the novel.

Your students who have reading difficulties, or speak English as a second language may benefit from listening to all or part of the book on tape. You may want to have some of your better readers, or a volunteer adult, make a tape of all or part of the book.

Other things you may keep on hand are word search puzzles. Several puzzles relating directly to *Flowers for Algernon* are included in the unit. Feel free to duplicate them.

Some students may like to draw. You might devise a contest or allow some extra-credit grade for students who draw characters or scenes from *Flowers for Algernon*. Note, too, that if the students do not want to keep their drawings you may pick up some extra bulletin board materials this way. If you have a contest and you supply the prize, you could, possibly, make the drawing itself a non-refundable entry fee.

The pages which follow contain games, puzzles, and worksheets. The keys, when appropriate, immediately follow the puzzle or worksheet. There are two main groups of activities: one group for the unit; that is, generally relating to the *Flowers for Algernon* text, and another group of activities related strictly to the *Flowers for Algernon* vocabulary.

Directions for the games, puzzles, and worksheets are self-explanatory. The object here is to provide you with extra materials you may use in any way you choose.

## MORE ACTIVITIES  *Flowers for Algernon*

1. Pick one of the incidents for students to dramatize. Encourage students to write dialog for the characters. (Perhaps you could assign various stories to different groups of students so more than one story could be acted and more students could participate.)

2. Have students design a book cover (front and back and inside flaps) for *Flowers for Algernon*.

3. Have students design a bulletin board (ready to be put up; not just sketched) for *Flowers for Algernon*.

4. Invite a story teller to tell one or more stories related to *Flowers for Algernon* to the class.

5. Use some of the related topics (noted earlier for an in-class library) as topics for research, reports, or written papers, or as topics for guest speakers.

6. Help students design and produce a talk show. Choose one of the story incidents as the topic. The host will interview the various characters. (Students should make up the questions they want the host to ask the characters.)

7. Have students work in pairs to create an interview with one of the characters. One student should be the interviewer and the other should be the interviewee. Students can work together to compose questions for the interviewer to ask. Each pair of students could present their interview to the class.

8. Invite students who have read other books by Daniel Keyes to present book talks to the class.

9. Invite students to build mazes out of cardboard or wood. If the school permits it, you may want to have someone bring a white mouse and watch it try to go through the maze.

10. Invite a local psychologist to talk to the class about the nature of intelligence, intelligence testing, and any work being done now that is designed to increase intelligence.

11. Have a speaker from an animal rights group talk to the class about the work he/she does.

12. Invite someone who has had experience with a mentally handicapped person to speak to the group.

13. Have students hold small group discussions related to topics in the book. Assign a recorder and a speaker for each group. Have the speaker from each group make a report to the class.

# WORD SEARCH *Flowers for Algernon*

All the words in this word search are associated with *Flowers for Algernon* with emphasis on the characters and events being studied in the unit. The words are placed backwards, forward, diagonally, up and down. The words used in the puzzle are listed below.

```
D K H R Q C V F B F M C P S U R F U M X H P M R E D R R G Q J V X M
P R M B Y N Q W X U W O J C E M V Q Z C F K S U I V E T E P B H V X
M R U P F P H W R R B C T I F J E M T I Q N T Z L J G I C N O X H E
I Q O N D F E R G V Q N L E A B M M L T O U R R R I R D V T N B R I
I S M G K O E O F Z O W Q N L G N P O N A N I A A B E B T E C O R Y
S V O K R B S K G X X Q U C K O S G R R H M E T H M S J W A F R D M
E K F E M E G D H K Q T J E F S Y E K B I C T U C Y S Q C C L G B O
Q Y D E C B S S M X A D O F E B G B A R B E R N R K E C F H A M E C
L R V G G Z J S K Z A K K X I T L N R M V S V S Y T O D E G E E K U A
J O W F P S W I R R B T Z C A P Q Z L Z T E Z A M D S Y G R P O F B
N A A L U M A F C E H I T T W B L U C U R G S F O F R U Y S L H O F
E V X N W G R V G G P W A I W D I J I E A H D Y U O Y N R C X S E T
I C Y T A E R P M O F O G O I Y C Z K Z U U A S T B X Z U G D V X E
B W I Z D A E Y T A G G R N L U R Y Y O S S R A F Q R O L P E F B S
P A G L T K N U Y E A Z J T X D R K Y P S O R C K B R U A M A O K U
F L K C A V Z W O C C G L Z H V U Q T F M O N I R A U G A I O B N L
N B C E K K D M J O L N G G P B M B K T B I I Z Q C Y U Z V B Z I M
P U H X R E O W M H Y H A H M A E V O A N X G P V D K P D G Q R R S
H R A W I Y R O S E H W P D T Y N H L S M A R C H M Y A P J M D H D
A T P D L Z S U Q E X Y S E S B I Q J V T R Z R O H E N Y Z P F S J
L H R U Q E X N S S F U I T B W E B D Q P I V U R Z K M O Y K G D Q
D O P B C P N S Q L H D C S P W G O R D O N R J N D C E C C B M D B
```

| | | |
|---|---|---|
| CHARLIE | GIMPY | GUARINO |
| ALICE | BARBER | DRUNK |
| NEMUR | WARREN | NEUROSURGEON |
| BURT | BAKERY | PROGRESS REPORT |
| ALGERNON | MEMORIES | MARCH |
| FAY | MAZE | NOVEMBER |
| STRAUSS | DANCE | DIED |
| DONNER | LABORATORY | REGRESSED |
| ROSE | SMART | GORDON |
| MATT | TEACHER | SCIENCE FICTION |

# CROSSWORD *Flowers for Algernon*

# CROSSWORD CLUES *Flowers for Algernon*

ACROSS
1 Charlie's pastime with Fay
5 What happened to Algernon
7 Charlie's feeling for Alice
8 Vehicle for telling the story; progress ___
9 Where Charlie worked
10 Mouse with increased intelligence
13 Shop Matt wanted to own
15 Administered inkblot and other tests
17 Algernon and Charlie competed at this
19 Author
22 Charlie's sister
24 An ordinary man trying to do a great man's work
25 Alice Kinnian's occupation
26 Charlie found them disturbing
27 Alice's last name

DOWN
1 What happened to artificially increased intelligence
2 Charlie's increased
3 Where Charlie wanted flowers for Algernon
4 Charlie's family name
5 Owner of bakery
6 Charlie and Algernon did this in Chicago
7 Where experiments were done
10 Teacher with whom Charlie fell in love
11 Stole from Mr. Donner
12 Inkblot test
13 College for Retarded Adults
14 Charlie's mother
16 Fay who was ful of life and excitement
17 Charlie's father
18 They gradually returned to Charlie
20 Foundation that provided money for experiment
21 What Charlie wanted to be
23 He said he was as good as Charlie

## CROSSWORD ANSWER KEY *Flowers for Algernon*

## MATCHING QUIZ 1 *Flowers for Algernon*

1. Algernon
2. bakery
3. Beekman
4. Charlie
5. Daniel Keys
6. died
7. dreams
8. escape
9. Frank
10. Gordon
11. Guarino
12. laboratory
13. March 3
14. maze
15. Nemur
16. November 21
17. science fiction
18. Strauss
19. Warren
20. Fay Lillman

A. full of life and excitement
B. psychiatrist and neurosurgeon
C. date of last progress report
D. Algernon and Charlie competed at this
E. where experiments were done
F. Charlie's family name
G. what Charlie and Algernon did in Chicago
H. what happened to Algernon
I. wanted to be smart to have people like him
J. where Charlie worked
K. State Home and Training School
L. genre of novel
M. " an ordinary man trying to do a great man's work"
N. date of first progress report
O. treated Charlie like a human being
P. said he was as good as Charlie
Q. Charlie found his disturbing
R. author
S. College for Retarded Adults
T. mouse with increased intelligence

## ANSWER KEY: MATCHING QUIZ 1 *Flowers for Algernon*

| | | | | | |
|---|---|---|---|---|---|
| T | 1. | Algernon | A. | full of life and excitement |
| J | 2. | bakery | B. | psychiatrist and neurosurgeon |
| S | 3. | Beekman | C. | date of last progress report |
| I | 4. | Charlie | D. | Algernon and Charlie competed at this |
| R | 5. | Daniel Keys | E. | where experiments were done |
| H | 6. | died | F. | Charlie's family name |
| Q | 7. | dreams | G. | what Charlie and Algernon did in Chicago |
| G | 8. | escape | H. | what happened to Algernon |
| P | 9. | Frank | I. | wanted to be smart to have people like him |
| F | 10. | Gordon | J. | where Charlie worked |
| O | 11. | Guarino | K. | State Home and Training School |
| E | 12. | laboratory | L. | genre of novel |
| N | 13. | March 3 | M. | " an ordinary man trying to do a great man's work" |
| D | 14. | maze | N. | date of first progress report |
| M | 15. | Nemur | O. | treated Charlie like a human being |
| C | 16. | November 21 | P. | said he was as good as Charlie |
| L | 17. | science fiction | Q. | Charlie found his disturbing |
| B | 18. | Strauss | R. | author |
| K | 19. | Warren | S. | College for Retarded Adults |
| A | 20. | Fay Lillman | T. | mouse with increased intelligence |

## MATCHING QUIZ 2 *Flowers for Algernon*

1. Alice Kinnian
2. barber
3. Burt Selden
4. dancing
5. deteriorated
6. Mr. Donner
7. drunk
8. Fay Lillman
9. Gimpy
10. grave
11. IQ
12. love
13. Matt
14. memories
15. Norma
16. operation
17. Rorschach
18. smart
19. Strauss
20. Warren

A. gradually returned to Charlie
B. teacher at Beekman College
C. how Charlie's intelligence increased
D. stole money from Mr. Donner
E. what Charlie wanted to be
F. bakery owner
G. didn't recognize his son
H. State Home and Training School
I. Charlie's condition at Mrs. Nemur's party
J. where Charlie wanted flowers for Algernon
K. artificially increased intelligence did this
L. administered tests
M. shop Matt wanted to own
N. Charlie's feeling for Alice
O. ink blot test
P. full of life and excitement
Q. Charlie's pastime with Fay
R. psychiatrist and neurosurgeon
S. Charlie's increased
T. Charlie's sister

## ANSWER KEY: MATCHING QUIZ 2 *Flowers for Algernon*

| | | | | | |
|---|---|---|---|---|---|
| B | 1. | Alice Kinnian | A. | gradually returned to Charlie |
| M | 2. | barber | B. | teacher at Beekman College |
| L | 3. | Burt Selden | C. | how Charlie's intelligence increased |
| Q | 4. | dancing | D. | stole money from Mr. Donner |
| K | 5. | deteriorated | E. | what Charlie wanted to be |
| F | 6. | Mr. Donner | F. | bakery owner |
| I | 7. | drunk | G. | didn't recognize his son |
| P | 8. | Fay Lillman | H. | State Home and Training School |
| D | 9. | Gimpy | I. | Charlie's condition at Mrs. Nemur's party |
| J | 10. | grave | J. | where Charlie wanted flowers for Algernon |
| S | 11. | IQ | K. | artificially increased intelligence did this |
| N | 12. | love | L. | administered tests |
| G | 13. | Matt | M. | shop Matt wanted to own |
| A | 14. | memories | N. | Charlie's feeling for Alice |
| T | 15. | Norma | O. | ink blot test |
| C | 16. | operation | P. | full of life and excitement |
| O | 17. | Rorschach | Q. | Charlie's pastime with Fay |
| E | 18. | smart | R. | psychiatrist and neurosurgeon |
| R | 19. | Strauss | S. | Charlie's increased |
| H | 20. | Warren | T. | Charlie's sister |

## JUGGLE LETTER REVIEW GAME *Flowers for Algernon*

| SCRAMBLED | WORD | CLUE |
|---|---|---|
| RLNGEAON | ALGERNON | mouse with increased intelligence |
| NAKALIINEINC | ALICE KINNIAN | teacher with whom Charlie fell in love |
| RAEBYK | BAKERY | where Charlie worked |
| RBARBE | BARBER | shop Matt wanted to own |
| EKMEANB | BEEKMAN | College for Retarded Adults |
| ESURDTLENB | BURT SELDEN | administered inkblot and other tests |
| RCEALIH | CHARLIE | wanted to be smart to have people like him |
| ADINGCN | DANCING | Charlie's pastime with Fay |
| LAENYIEKESD | DANIEL KEYES | author |
| REEATOREDIT | DETERIORATE | artificially increased intelligence does this |
| IDED | DIED | what happened to Algernon |
| NODERN | DONNER | owner of bakery |
| ADMESR | DREAMS | Charlie found them disturbing |
| RDNKU | DRUNK | Charlie's condition at Mrs. Nemur's party |
| SEAPECP | ESCAPE | Charlie and Algernon did this in Chicago |
| NLFYIMALAL | FAY LILLMAN | full of life and excitement |
| KRFNA | FRANK | said he was as good as Charlie |
| PIGMY | GIMPY | stole from Mr. Donner |
| DROGNO | GORDON | Charlie's family name |
| VEGAR | GRAVE | Charlie wanted flowers for Algernon here |
| RAINOGU | GUARINO | Dr. who treated Charlie like a human being |
| LROOARAYBT | LABORATORY | where experiments were done |
| VELO | LOVE | Charlie's feeling for Alice |
| TATM | MATT | Charlie's father |
| ZAEM | MAZE | Algernon beat Charlie at this |
| EMOESRIM | MEMORIES | gradually returned to Charlie |
| RENUM | NEMUR | ordinary man doing a great man's work" |
| ROMAN | NORMA | Charlie's sister |
| OARTONPEI | OPERATION | how Charlie's intelligence increases |
| CRORSCAHH | RORSCHACH | inkblot test |
| ECINSEC | SCIENCE | novel is this type of fiction |
| MASTR | SMART | what Charlie wanted to be |
| STSARUS | STRAUSS | psychiatrist and neurosurgeon |
| RACHETE | TEACHER | Alice Kinnian's occupation |
| RAWENR | WARREN | State Home and Training School |
| BELEWGR | WELBERG | Foundation that supported experiment |

# VOCABULARY RESOURCES

# VOCABULARY WORD SEARCH
*Flowers for Algernon*

All the words in this list are associated with Flowers for Algernon with emphasis on the vocabulary words being studied in the unit. The words are placed backwards, forward, diagonally, up and down. The included words are listed below the word search.

```
D L W J I S K S N H I U A D D B O V Y C B Q X Y R G W S W B V N Y P X
D E U F O J N Z K A N P H S K E K D N X I V P D R A K X B A J G G R Z
H E T M I I P O F R S O B U J A S B W Z C J B O C A U I Z O B Q L Z X
W H G A I O L U I K X G I D N E U P O X O I N T U I T I O N I R C W O
B F B E L N D A J T L Z E T I C E G I A W H P W L D Z P O S O W T I A
P E T C N U E B X J A D P W C N H P U S B Z J Z I M Z P V X G M M R M
J G I I V E M S C R B G X A C U S E E P I F F L K P X P N W N S R O V
B I K T M S R U C N D V I O T O R S S L Q N A D N G Z A K U P W X B Q
L E R N A M M A C E S P M L I H Y T A R B V G Z S M N I M Z L Y W X H
I Z P E N J H Y T C N P K Q B W O N S Q K S F D Z B J B I K C G T G O
H V O R Y P H A U E A T R S K O J L S B U Q J L G D E H W I N M R P H
B E I P H Z L L S S G H K C P R V J O P O T L X A Q O M D F Y Y N T L
H J F P Y O P O S F X B B I N X E J E G Q B S X Z I P F N S B M N N B
Y M T A S L P I Z V F J U T K C P R L W Y Z U W G R L W V T S I I H Q
D J P I A R N Z K D E C F S V O I J S L J C Q N S E E K X H R M H G G
M N D T Y G L A C I N Y C C D M W N N C F Q Q P T C K U E Y Z S T D X
L G E Z J N L F M D U O U W P P E S M B V J L A P E F A B Z R N A M P
K A N G O K N Q U T X T U O E O U F D Z U A V C W D M A J K G Q L L H
U H Y X R K S U L G D H S S D S G W P Y I T Y X D E L I K U B N J Q X
G N V E S L U P M I U E V C H U A O S D I G P U C L A O R Z D Z E J N
M P E C U O L X X S D E G L P R V D R K V Q U N O E E W Z N G K C Q Z
X D N J Q F I S C V S Z S Y V E W O Q E F P M L Y F Y M I B L T K P C
W S N P R E A G B L Z N I V F B C Y E A I G C P D W G V A T K L H I Q
```

| | | |
|---|---|---|
| ACCUMULATED | FUGUES | OBLIGATIONS |
| APPRENTICE | HUNCHES | OBSTRUCTION |
| COMPOSURE | IMPULSE | PATHOLOGY |
| CORDIAL | INTUITION | PLATEAU |
| CYNICAL | ISOLATED | RECEDE |
| DEGENERATE | LABYRINTH | SUPERIMPOSED |
| DESPISING | LUMINESCENT | VAGUE |
| ENCOMPASSING | NUMB | VALID |
| FLAIL | | |

# VOCABULARY CROSSWORD *Flowers for Algernon*

# VOCABULARY CROSSWORD CLUES *Flowers for Algernon*

## ACROSS
1 To strike or lash out violently
2 Knowing or sensing without rational processes
8 A steady lowering of quality
11 Indistinctly felt, perceived, or understood
13 Irregular; not uniform
15 Given out; dispensed
23 State of sluggishness or inactivity
25 Disliking intensely
26 Cringes in fear
27 Try to prevent

## DOWN
1 Having no useful result
3 The state of being unaware of something that most people know; innocence
4 Something hinted or suggested
5 Unresponsive; unfeeling
6 Amnesiac conditions
7 Large
8 Corrupt; wicked
9 To move back or away from
10 Something in the way
11 Entrance hall
12 A maze
14 Surrounding
15 One who is learning a trade or occupation
16 Abandoned or isolated with little hope of rescue
17 Yielding to supervision or management
18 To reprimand gently but earnestly
19 State of mental numbness
20 Expressing scorn and bitter mockery
21 Contrary to what was expected or intended
22 True; correct
24 Partial or total loss of memory

## VOCABULARY CROSSWORD ANSWER KEY *Flowers for Algernon*

## VOCABULARY WORKSHEET 1  *Flowers for Algernon*

_____ 1. accumulated          A. to reprove gently but earnestly
_____ 2. admonish             B. a depraved or corrupt person
_____ 3. apprentice           C. placement side by side for comparison
_____ 4. complicated          D. the state of being artless or uncritical
_____ 5. conscious            E. one who is learning a trade or occupation
_____ 6. consistent           F. yielding to supervision or direction
_____ 7. cowers               G. seemingly contradictory but possibly true
_____ 8. degenerate           H. that which is hinted at or suggested
_____ 9. despising            I. disliking intensely; loathing
_____ 10. docile              J. gathered or piled up
_____ 11. erratic             K. to strike or lash out violently
_____ 12. flail               L. not easy to understand or analyze
_____ 13. imperceptibly       M. a maze
_____ 14. implication         N. reliable or uniform
_____ 15. ironic              O. contrary to what is expected or intended
_____ 16. juxtaposition       P. waking awareness perceptible by a person
_____ 17. labyrinth           Q. emitting light
_____ 18. luminescent         R. lacking consistency, regularity, or uniformity
_____ 19. naïveté             S. cringes in fear
_____ 20. paradoxical         T. not aware of

# ANSWER KEY VOCABULARY WORKSHEET 1 *Flowers for Algernon*

| | | | | | |
|---|---|---|---|---|---|
| J | 1. | accumulated | A. | to reprove gently but earnestly |
| A | 2. | admonish | B. | a depraved or corrupt person |
| E | 3. | apprentice | C. | placement side by side for comparison |
| L | 4. | complicated | D. | the state of being artless or uncritical |
| P | 5. | conscious | E. | one who is learning a trade or occupation |
| N | 6. | consistent | F. | yielding to supervision or direction |
| S | 7. | cowers | G. | seemingly contradictory but possibly true |
| B | 8. | degenerate | H. | that which is hinted at or suggested |
| I | 9. | despising | I. | disliking intensely; loathing |
| F | 10. | docile | J. | gathered or piled up |
| R | 11. | erratic | K. | to strike or lash out violently |
| K | 12. | flail | L. | not easy to understand or analyze |
| T | 13. | imperceptibly | M. | a maze |
| H | 14. | implication | N. | reliable or uniform |
| O | 15. | ironic | O. | contrary to what is expected or intended |
| C | 16. | juxtaposition | P. | waking awareness perceptible by a person |
| M | 17. | labyrinth | Q. | emitting light |
| Q | 18. | luminescent | R. | lacking consistency, regularity, or uniformity |
| D | 19. | naïveté | S. | cringes in fear |
| G | 20. | paradoxical | T. | not aware of |

## VOCABULARY WORKSHEET 2 *Flowers for Algernon*

____ 1. **a calm or tranquil state of mind**
    A. lethargy    B. composure    C. plateau    D. stupor

____ 2. **diminishing in quality**
    A. juxtaposition    B. queasy    C. deterioration    D. valid

____ 3. **surrounding**
    A. encompassing    B. usurped    C. complicated    D. inevitable

____ 4. **mild terms that are substituted for offensive ones**
    A. cowers    B. prognosis    C. exigencies    D. euphemisms

____ 5. **amnesiac conditions**
    A. pompous    B. fugues    C. naïveté    D. obligations

____ 6. **assumes a crouched or cramped posture**
    A. recede    B. luminescent    C. ornately    D. hunches

____ 7. **knowing or sensing without rational processes**
    A. conscious    B. procedure    C. skeptical    D. intuition

____ 8. **set apart or cut off from others**
    A. isolated    B. accumulated    C. erratic    D. depraved

____ 9. **large or imposing**
    A. berserk    B. docile    C. massive    D. ironic

____ 10. **a departure or deviation from a normal condition**
    A. amnesia    B. pathology    C. cynical    D. futile

____ 11. **unusual or eccentric; odd**
    A. complicated    B. imperceptibly    C. platonic    D. peculiar

____ 12. **extraordinary; outstanding**
    A. phenomenal    B. skeptical    C. superimposed    D. permanent

____ 13. **spiritual or ideal and not physical**
    A. queasy    B. platonic    C. valid    D. pompous

____ 14. **an action taken in advance to protect against possible danger**
    A. vestibule    B. labyrinth    C. precaution    D. procedure

____ 15. **a prediction of the probable course and outcome of a disease**
    A. juxtaposition    B. apprentice    C. prognosis    D. implication

____ 16. **marked by doubt; questioning**
    A. skeptical    B. conscious    C. composure    D. intuition

____ 17. **placed on or over something else**
    A. administered    B. erratic    C. encompassing    D. superimposed

____ 18. **producing the desired results**
    A. complicated    B. valid    C. accumulated    D. vague

____ 19. **a small entrance hall between the outer door and the interior of a house**
    A. deterioration    B. exigencies    C. vestibule    D. impulse

____ 20. **to try to prevent**
    A. ward    B. flail    C. cowers    D. despising

## ANSWER KEY VOCABULARY WORKSHEET 2 *Flowers for Algernon*

**B** 1. **a calm or tranquil state of mind**
   A. lethargy    B. **composure**    C. plateau    D. stupor

**C** 2. **diminishing in quality**
   A. juxtaposition    B. queasy    C. **deterioration**    D. valid

**A** 3. **surrounding**
   A. **encompassing**    B. usurped    C. complicated    D. inevitable

**D** 4. **mild terms that are substituted for offensive ones**
   A. cowers    B. prognosis    C. exigencies    D. **euphemisms**

**B** 5. **amnesiac conditions**
   A. pompous    B. **fugues**    C. naïveté    D. obligations

**D** 6. **assumes a crouched or cramped posture**
   A. recede    B. luminescent    C. ornately    D. **hunches**

**D** 7. **knowing or sensing without rational processes**
   A. conscious    B. procedure    C. skeptical    D. **intuition**

**A** 8. **set apart or cut off from others**
   A. **isolated**    B. accumulated    C. erratic    D. depraved

**C** 9. **large or imposing**
   A. berserk    B. docile    C. **massive**    D. ironic

**B** 10. **a departure or deviation from a normal condition**
   A. amnesia    B. **pathology**    C. cynical    D. futile

**D** 11. **unusual or eccentric; odd**
   A. complicated    B. imperceptibly    C. platonic    D. **peculiar**

**A** 12. **extraordinary; outstanding**
   A. **phenomenal**    B. skeptical    C. superimposed    D. permanent

**B** 13. **spiritual or ideal and not physical**
   A. queasy    B. **platonic**    C. valid    D. pompous

**C** 14. **an action taken in advance to protect against possible danger**
   A. vestibule    B. labyrinth    C. **precaution**    D. procedure

**C** 15. **a prediction of the probable course and outcome of a disease**
   A. juxtaposition    B. apprentice    C. **prognosis**    D. implication

**A** 16. **marked by doubt; questioning**
   A. **skeptical**    B. conscious    C. composure    D. intuition

**D** 17. **placed on or over something else**
   A. administered    B. erratic    C. encompassing    D. **superimposed**

**B** 18. **producing the desired results**
   A. complicated    B. **valid**    C. accumulated    D. vague

**C** 19. **a small entrance hall between the outer door and the interior of a house**
   A. deterioration    B. exigencies    C. **vestibule**    D. impulse

**A** 20. **to try to prevent**
   A. **ward**    B. flail    C. cowers    D. despising

## VOCABULARY JUGGLE LETTER REVIEW GAME *Flowers for Algernon*

| SCRAMBLED | WORD | CLUE |
|---|---|---|
| NDHOMISA | ADMONISH | to reprove gently but earnestly |
| NAMEIAS | AMNESIA | partial or total loss of memory |
| REEKBSR | BERSERK | destructively or frenetically violent |
| SCOURPOEM | COMPOSURE | a calm or tranquil state of mind |
| DRALOCI | CORDIAL | warm and sincere; friendly |
| WORESC | COWERS | cringes in fear |
| LYICCAN | CYNICAL | expressing scorn and bitter mockery |
| VDPEAEDR | DEPRAVED | corrupt, wicked |
| EOILCD | DOCILE | yielding to supervision or direction |
| TRECRAI | ERRATIC | lacking consistency, or regularity |
| LFAIL | FLAIL | to strike or lash out violently |
| GUFUSE | FUGUES | amnesiac conditions |
| UVLITEF | FUTILE | having no useful result |
| CENHHSU | HUNCHES | assumes a crouched or cramped posture |
| MIPUELS | IMPULSE | sudden urge that prompts an action |
| IUTINONVI | INTUITION | knowing without rational processes |
| NIOICR | IRONIC | contrary to what was expected |
| DIALTOES | ISOLATED | set apart or cut off from others |
| VASEMIS | MASSIVE | large or imposing |
| TOYRAELN | ORNATELY | flashy or showy in style or manner |
| CLEPIARU | PECULIAR | unusual or eccentric; odd |
| TULAEPA | PLATEAU | a stable level, period, or state |
| ALPONCIT | PLATONIC | spiritual or ideal and not physical |
| MOUSPOP | POMPOUS | excessive self-esteem |
| USAYEQ | QUEASY | causing nausea; sickening |
| EEDECR | RECEDE | to move back or away from a limit |
| EIPSCAKLT | SKEPTICAL | marked by or given to doubt |
| RPTOSU | STUPOR | mental numbness, |
| RSOOGPNIS | PROGNOSIS | prediction of a disease's course |
| RUPSUDE | USURPED | taken over or occupied without right |
| GEAUV | VAGUE | indistinctly felt, perceived, understood |
| DVAIL | VALID | producing the desired results |
| DRAW | WARD | to try to prevent |

www.ingramcontent.com/pod-product-compliance
Lightning Source LLC
LaVergne TN
LVHW081537060526
838200LV00048B/2106